The 55 WEST VIRGINIAS

The
55 WEST VIRGINIAS

A Guide to the State's Counties

E. Lee North

Second and Revised Edition

John Luchok, Editor
Todd M. Yeager, Historical Review Editor

West Virginia University Press
Morgantown
1998

Published by the West Virginia University Press, Morgantown, WV 26506-6069
Copyright© E. Lee North
All rights reserved
Manufactured in the United States of America

International Standard Book Number
0-937058-38-6

Library of Congress Number 97-60500

Cover: Mountains of Monongahela National Forest rise around Parsons, Tucker County seat. *(L. Victor Haines, WVU Photographic Services)*

Inside front cover: State Capitol complex on the Kanawha River. *(L. Victor Haines, WVU Photographic Services)*

Inside back cover: Historic Harpers Ferry, Lowest point in West Virginia at 247 feet above sea level, where the Potomac and Shenandoah Rivers come together. *(L. Victor Haines, WVU Photographic Services)*

Dedication

For my wife Florence, my son Patrick, and my daughter Diane— all born in West Virginia— and their families, and to my mother, Jean North Francais, and brother Dick—ex-West Virginians. And Judy Herndon (I never knew her, but hoped she would become the first female governor of West Virginia).

I also dedicate this Second Edition to the Hennen and Haning clans of Wheeling— they've been wonderful in-laws, nieces, and nephews over the years. A special thanks to Atwood Haning, Anna Marie Fouts, Susie Britt, and Mary Hamm for their Ohio County inputs.

To The Governors

A salute to Cecil H. Underwood, a Tyler County native elected the youngest governor of West Virginia in 1956, and the oldest in 1996. He was 34 years old in '56, and 74 years old in 1996. Good Luck, Governor (and Mrs. Hovah) Underwood!

And congratulations to outgoing Governor Gaston Caperton, who is credited by both major parties with improving the state's economy and image. Caperton served two terms, 1989-97. Good Luck, Gaston and Rachael, in whatever you do!

About the Author

E. Lee North is also the author of *Redcoats, Redskins, and Red-Eyed Monsters,* a human interest history of West Virginia published by A.S. Barnes, Inc.; *She Produces All-Americans,* a history of football at his alma mater, Washington & Jefferson College; and a novel, *For This One Hour,* set in Poland and Russia during World War II. He was editor of the W & J undergraduate weekly, *The Red and Black,* for two years and a member of the History and Journalism national honor societies. After serving as sports editor of the *Washington Reporter* and publicity director at W & J, North worked as editor and proposal manager at Grumman Aerospace for 37 years, retiring in 1989.

In 1991, North completed a history of W & J's century of football (1890-1990), *Battling the Indians, Panthers, and Nittany Lions.* Published by Daring Books of Canton, Ohio, *Battling* includes much about West Virginia schools and players, as WVU was one of W & J's top opponents from the 1890s into the 1930s. The Presidents have also played West Virginia Wesleyan, Fairmont, Marshall, and Bethany— the latter still W & J's No. 1 rival in number of games played to 1997.

North's latest literary efforts are two books for which he is co-author: *Chris, the Rhode Island Wonder Dog* (with Jane Wyman), published in 1993 at Western New England College; and *The History of Bay Shore (LI) High School Athletics* (with Arthur Dromerhauser), published in 1994 by GMG Graphics of New York City. He is a member of the Authors Guild and the Football Writers of America.

Author's Tribute to Jim Comstock

Dear Mrs. Comstock, and the staff of Jim's beloved *Hillbilly,*

My heart grieves. West Virginia and the Nation have lost a great man, a wonderful writer, and an accomplished historian. More, we have all lost a dear friend.

Florence and I extend our sincere sympathies to all of you who knew Jim so well, and of course mostly to you, Ola— so often referred to in Jim's loving way as the "Poor wretch" who had to put up with him and his antics. And of course, to all those of your and Jim's wonderful family.

When I started work on a West Virginia history in the 1960's, Jim was right there with copies of the *Hillbilly*— sent dozens of them to me and never asked for a cent. And what a source of history they were! Nothing can compare, not even the WV Historical Society bulletins, which seemed to come out whenever someone felt like it. Jim also offered any personal help he could give, and he was the one primarily responsible for our work that was published by A.S. Barnes— *Redcoats, Redskins, and Red-Eyed Mosters* some fifteen years ago.

As you West Virginians know so well, Jim didn't waste any time. Remember the history room he had upstairs in the old *Hillbilly* building? He took me up there one day and I acquired some books for my research. On the way down (also, remember how narrow, steep, and worn the stairs were?), I slipped and fell to the bottom with a wrenched knee. Jim looked at me lying there and said, "What did you do that for!" He extended a hand, pulled me up, and he was out the door (we were on our way to one of his inveterate coffee clatches). I had no choice but to drag myself out the door and catch up. Jim wasn't the type who would mope around feeling sorry for you (or himself)!

And of course when we had coffee with the others, he seldom sat still (or remained quiet). He was on the trail of a story all the time. As most WV'ans know, he wrote or proof-read furiously while Ola (or another designated driver) drove him to whatever meeting or event that captured his fancy. And what stories he told! Over thirty-odd years, I never read one that did not hold my complete interest. I really hope Sandy will run them forever on the *Hillbilly's* back page (as a continuing "Comstock Load").— Sandy, what say?

A few nights ago, I dreamt about Jim and woke up with a start. I realized he'd not produced anything for *Hillbilly's* back page lately and feared the worst. The next morning (may have been two), there was Jim's obit— about a quarter of a page!— in the NY Times. Florence (my native WV'an nee Hennen of Wheeling) and I were deeply saddened, for we have read Comstockisms lo, these three-plus decades. What will we all do now?

I'd not be surprised to see Jim's byline popping up again— I don't see how Heaven will be able to slow him down.

Your friend,

Sincerely,

E. Lee North (and Florence H. North)

P.S. All *Hillbilly* readers: Let this *Hillbilly* newspaper be a shining monument to Jim— let's get more and more people to subscribe to this great source of West Virginiana!

Preface

Come now, you might ask, *fifty-five* West Virginias?

In support of the claim, we ask you to consider the West Virginia of the Northern Panhandle, stretching as it does north of Pittsburgh. More like Pennsylvania and Ohio. And consider the Eastern Panhandle, reaching to within forty miles of Washington, D.C., and holding apart Maryland and Virginia in the process. Many of its people still lament the fact that it ever broke away from Virginia and, indeed, the area's orchards and towns remind one of the Old Dominion.

Then there's the West Virginia of Logan, Mingo, and Wayne counties, stretching west of Port Huron, Michigan, and acting more like Kentucky. Here the Hatfields and McCoys fought the most famous family feud in the world. And there's the West Virginia of the southern tier, with the mountains around Bluefield reaching south of Richmond and reminding one more of Tennessee and North Carolina. North, south, east, and west are thus well represented . . . but there's more. Take a trip to the heights of Snowshoe and the imposing mountains of Pocahontas, Tucker, and Randolph counties and be amazed to think yourself in Canada or New England. Then there's the sleepy, restful quiet of the Back Fork of the Elk in Webster County, with high mountains on either side keeping the sun at bay. Sweep down the Ohio past Pleasants, Wood, Jackson, and Mason counties to aptly named Point Pleasant.

Ah, you might point out, but these are *regions* . . . aren't the counties of the Northern Panhandle— Hancock, Brooke, Ohio, and Marshall— for example, quite the same? Well, each of these has its own most unique and engaging history. Hancock, named for the first signer of the Declaration of Independence, is the northernmost county in the state and the site of the beginning of the surveying of the public lands of the United States (September 30, 1785). Brooke County and Bethany were the home of Alexander Campbell, who founded the Disciples of Christ Church here in 1809 and Bethany College, oldest private college in the state, in 1840. Moving down the river, Ohio County boasts one of the most interesting histories of any county in the country. Its leading city, Wheeling, was for several years in the nineteenth century the largest town in the United States west of Philadelphia. It was also the site of Fort Henry and what has been called the last battle of the American Revolution; the birthplace of the state; and its first capital. Finally, the southernmost of the panhandle counties, Marshall, is the home of a famous Indian burial mound. This truly impressive mound— sixty-nine feet high and almost a thousand feet in circumference— gives the name to the county's principal city, Moundsville. This county was the scene of completion of the first great railroad in history, the Baltimore and Ohio— at Rossby's Rock where the east and west tracks were joined in 1852.

Of course, we've only touched the surface of a few of the state's county histories. There's still another West Virginia— a fifty-sixth, one might say. It's in Kanawha County, and its center is Charleston, capital of the state. Here all the counties come together via the state's elected representatives. And here you'll find that, despite all the differences in area and topography, there's that other West Virginia, one of which its people are extremely proud. And these people are among the friendliest, yet most independent, in the United States. Their history could be described as incredible, but the word seems inadequate.

Contents

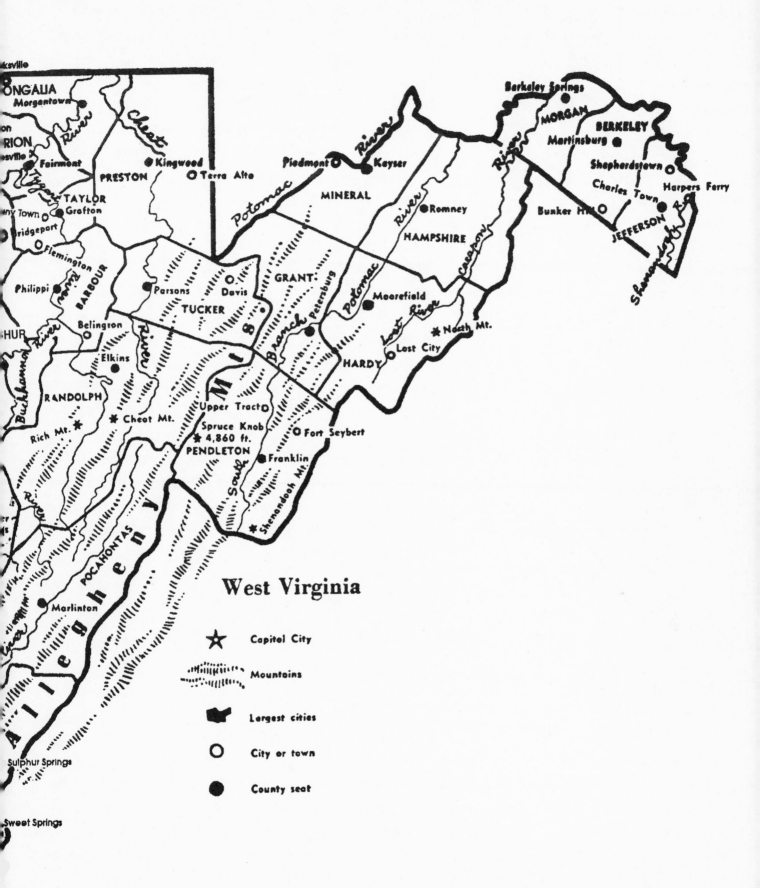

West Virginia

★   Capitol City

Mountains

Largest cities

○   City or town

●   County seat

The
55 WEST VIRGINIAS

Barbour County

(West Virginia and Regional History Collection, WVU Libraries)

Barbour County is located in the north-central part of the state upon the Appalachian plateau. The land is hilly to mountainous and is drained by the Tygart, Buckhannon, and Middle Fork rivers. The first settlements within what is now Barbour County were made as early as 1780 near present-day Philippi. In 1843, Barbour County was formed from parts of Randolph, Lewis, and Harrison counties. It was named for Phillip Pendleton Barbour (1783-1841), a distinguished Virginia jurist. By 1850 it had a population of 9,005. What is generally regarded as the first land battle of the Civil War took place in Barbour County. The relatively minor skirmish occurred on June 3, 1861, when Federal troops under General B. F. Kelley defeated Confederate forces under Colonel George A. Porterfield.

Spanning the Tygart River at Philippi is the old covered bridge, one of West Virginia's historic landmarks. Designed by Lemuel Chenoweth, it was built in 1852. The bridge has been strengthened to permit modern traffic loads to pass through it.

Barbour County has always been predominantly an agricultural and grazing county, with most of its farms located along the river valleys. Livestock, fruit, and poultry are some of the agricultural products of the county. The county's coal, lumber, gas, and oil reserves were exploited soon after the completion of the rail transportation system in the closing decades of the 19th century. Coal production began in 1894 when the mines of the county produced 8,664 tons. Production rose to 2,873,705 tons in 1920 and peaked in 1948 at 3,895,803 tons. In 1980, coal production totaled 3,659,000 tons,

about one-half from surface mines. The population of the county was 18,028 in 1920; it peaked in 1940 at 19,869, and declined to 14,030 in 1970. In 1990, it was 15,699.

Philippi, the county seat, was established in 1844 and named for Phillip Pendleton Barbour. It was originally known as Booth's Ferry or Anglin's Ford. Its' population was 1,543 in 1920; by 1990 it had risen to 3,132. Alderson-Broaddus College, located at Philippi, was established in 1901 as a result of the union of two earlier schools-—Broaddus Female College, formerly located at Clarksburg, and Alderson Academy, formerly located at Alderson.

ECONOMIC PROFILE

Poverty status	
(all persons)	28.5%
65 and older	22.2%
Farms/value of farm products sold	459/$3.69 million
Retail sales	$43.94 million
Home ownership	77.5%
Value added by mining	$40.2 million
Median home value	$35,200
Median rent	$177/mo.

Barbour County Notables

Ida L. Reed, Composer of hundreds of hymns, including "I Belong to the King."

Howard Willis Smith (1894-1992). Artist, cartoonist, successful businessman.

Bibliography

Barbour County Historical Society, *Barbour County, West Virginia, . . . Another Look.* Philippi, 1979.

Maxwell, Hu. *The History of Barbour County, West Virginia, From its Earliest Exploration and Settlement to the Present Time.* Morgantown, Acme Publishing Co., 1899. Reprinted: Parsons, McClain Printing Co., 1968.

BARBOUR COUNTY

Land in square miles	343
Total population	15,699
Percentage rural	80.0
Percentage female population	52.2
Percentage African-American population	0.9
Median age	34.9
Birth rate per 1,000 pop.	12.1
Percentage 65 and older	16.0
Median family income	$19,106

Educational attainment

Percent high school graduate or higher	59.8
Percent bachelor's degree or higher	10.1

Berkeley County

Morgan Morgan, first white settler in West Virginia, originally built this home in 1731-34 in an area that became known as Torytown. The house was rebuilt with some of the original logs in 1976. (L. Victor Haines, WVU Photographic Services)

Berkeley County lies in the center of the Eastern Panhandle of the state, and is one of the counties comprising what was once known as the Northern Neck of Virginia. It is situated in the Ridge and Valley province of the Appalachian mountain system, and is drained by the Potomac River. The first permanent settlement in what is now West Virginia is generally credited to Morgan Morgan, who settled at Bunker Hill in this county in the early 1730's.

The first Episcopal church in the state was founded by Morgan Morgan, Joist Hite, and John Briscoe in 1740. Berkeley County also claims the first Baptist church in the state—Mill Creek Church—organized in 1745 at Gerardstown. In 1748, Lord Fairfax, the English nobleman who inherited a vast tract of land on the Potomac basin that included present-day Berkeley County, sent a team of surveyors, including George Washington, to this "Western Country" to divide the land into manors and lots. The rich limestone soil attracted many settlers, and by 1772 the area was sufficiently populated to bring about the formation of Berkeley County from the northern third of Frederick County, Virginia. The county was named for Norborne Berkeley (Baron de Botetourt), Colonial Governor of Virginia from 1768 to 1770, and is the second oldest county in the state.

Berkeley County developed a diversified agricultural economy in the antebellum period. The 1850 Census shows that the 11,771 people in the county produced wheat, rye, corn, oats, potatoes, and livestock. With its many "watering places" the county was also an attractive tourist spot during this era when mineral springs were in vogue. The coming of the Baltimore and Ohio Railroad, passing through Martinsburg in 1842, brought a stimulus to the economic development of the county, and by 1860 Martinsburg was, next to Wheeling, the largest city in what is now the state of West Virginia.

During the Civil War, Berkeley County was a virtual no-man's land. Although there were no major battles in the county, there were numerous raids and skirmishes. Martinsburg changed hands no less than ten times during the war. The B & O line suffered repeated raids early in the war at the hands of the Southern armies led by General Thomas (Stonewall) Jackson.

Berkeley County was not included in the state of West Virginia at the time of its admission to the Union on June 20, 1863, but in July of that same year, Governor Pierpont certified that a large majority of voters were in favor of becoming part of the state and it was admitted. Berkeley County remained a quiet rural area until after World War II. In recent years greatly improved transportation and the natural charm and beauty of the region have combined to make the county increasingly attractive to light industry and residents of other states. As a result Berkeley has grown rapidly in both wealth and population. Indeed, the population increased from 36,356 in 1970 to 46,775 in 1980, a gain of 28.7 percent and rose again in 1990 to over 59,000.

Martinsburg, the county seat, was settled by English and German colonists between 1732 and 1776. In 1778, General Adam Stephen, who fought in the Revolutionary War, laid out the town on land bought from the Fairfax estate and named it for Col. T. B. Martin, a nephew of Lord Fairfax. The city has been graced by an unusual number of fine homes; many of these have been well preserved and attract many visitors. The city had a population of 14,073 in 1990.

Berkeley County Notables

Newton D. Baker (1871-1937). Lawyer and US Secretary of War, 1916-1921.

Belle Boyd (1843-1900). Confederate spy and actress.

Admiral Richard E. Byrd (1888-1957). Famous explorer, first person to fly over North and South poles.

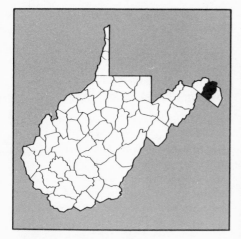

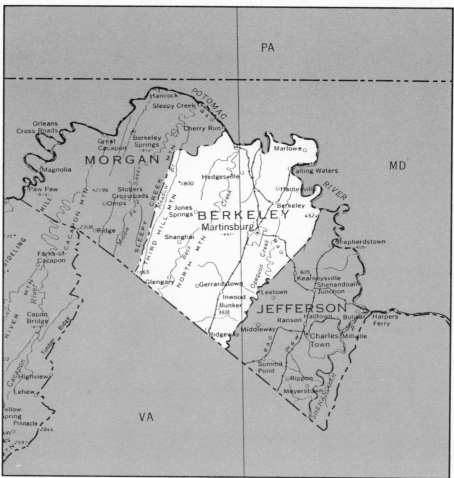

ECONOMIC PROFILE

Poverty status (all persons)	12.0%
65 and older	15.7%
Farms/value of farm products sold	453/$18.81 million
Retail sales	$287.74 million
Home ownership	73.0%
Value added by mining	NA
Median home value	$70,600
Median rent	$284/mo.

Harry Flood Byrd (1887-1966). Born in Martinsburg, served as US Senator from Virginia, 1933-65, and as Governor, 1926-30.

Charles J. Faulkner (1806-1884). Member of Congress and Minister to France.

Charles J. Faulkner, Jr. (1847-1929). Lawyer and United States Senator, 1887-1899.

A Willis Robertson (1887-1971) born in Martinsburg, served as US Senator from Virginia, 1846-67.

David H. Strother (1816-1888). Author and soldier. He wrote under the name of Porte Crayon.

Louis R. "Hack" Wilson (1900-1948). Baseball player who set several National League batting records.

Bibliography

Aler, F. Vernon. *Aler's History of Martinsburg and Berkeley County, West Virginia.* Hagerstown, 1888.

Doherty, William T. *Berkeley County USA: A Bicentennial History.* Parsons, McClain Printing Co., 1972.

Evans, Willis F. *History of Berkeley County, West Virginia.* Martinsburg, 1928.

BERKELEY COUNTY

Land in square miles	322
Total Population	59,253
Percentage rural	75.0
Percentage female population	50.3
Percentage African-American population	3.7
Median age	33.3
Birth rate per 1,000 pop.	15.5
Percentage 65 and older	11.8
Median family income	$32,040

Educational attainment

Percent high school graduate or higher	68.4
Percent bachelor's degree or higher	11.9

Boone County

Coal cars at Danville, with Madison in background. *(Joe Linville Photography)*

1970 to 1980, but the total dipped to about 26,000 in 1990.

Danville, incorporated in 1911 and named for its first postmaster, Dan Rock, was formerly known as Newport and Red House.

Madison, the county seat, was incorporated in 1906, and by 1910 had a population of 295. The name of the town has been the subject of some dispute. Some feel that it was named after Col. William Madison Peyton, a pioneer coal operator of the era; others maintain that it was named after Madison Laidley, a Charleston attorney and advisor to the county. In 1980 Madison had a population of 3,228.

Peytona, the site of an Indian burial ground dating to about 1400 AD, and Buck Garden, dating to 1000 AD.

Whitesville, incorporated in 1935 and named for an early settler, D. B. White, was formerly known as Jarrold's Valley and Pritchard City. An incredible tragedy struck the town in the early 1900s when a footbridge collapsed as people rushed on it to view a vaudeville act; some 85 people were killed.

Boone County is situated in the southwestern part of the state. The Big Coal and Little Coal rivers flow through the county, which was formed in 1857 from parts of Kanawha, Cabell, and Logan counties. It was named for Daniel Boone, the noted hunter and explorer who lived in the Kanawha Valley for several years and represented the area in the Virginia General Assembly. The first recorded visit of whites was in 1742 when John Peter Salling (Salley) led an exploration party to the area. He named Coal River for the abundance of coal visible at Racine. It was the first recorded discovery of coal in what was to become one of the nation's top coal-producing states.

In the 1840's and '50's, the Big Coal River was made navigable past Marsh Fork. However, a flood destroyed the lock and dam system in 1884, and it played only a small role in the economy of the area.

Boone County was very thinly populated during its early years. The rugged terrain and poor transportation made the area unattractive to settlers. As late as 1890 the population of the county was less than 7,000. However, the growing demand for coal induced capitalists to build railroads and open mines. The State Department of Mines first reported coal production in Boone County in 1909—a grand total of 3,451 tons. Both coal production and the resulting population grew rapidly. By 1960 production was over six million tons and by 1980 almost fourteen million tons. Population increased to over 15,000 by 1920 and peaked at 33,173 in 1950. Another increase in population took place from

Boone County Notables
Leonard S. Echols (1871-1946). Member of the US House of Representatives, 1919-23.

Sigfus Olafson (1896-1989). Respected state archaeologist.

Billy Edd Wheeler (1930-). Playwright and composer.

John M. Zontini (1909-1981). All-state in football at Sherman (Seth) HS, then one of Marshall University's all-time greats.

Bibliography
"Boone County Edition." *West Virginia Review* 19:6. March 1942.

Scott, Eugene L. "Whitesville." *West Virginia Review* 24:2, p. 22-24. Nov. 1946.

ECONOMIC PROFILE

Poverty status (all persons)	27.0%
65 and older	18.2%
Farms/value of farm products sold	31/$53,000
Retail sales	$104.67 million
Home ownership	76.3%
Value added by mining	$519.6 million
Median home value	$41,800
Median rent	$196/mo.

BOONE COUNTY

Land in square miles	503
Total population	25,870
Percentage rural	88.2
Percentage female population	51.4
Percentage African-American population	0.8
Median age	34.5
Birth rate per 1,000 pop.	13.9
Percentage 65 and older	12.6
Median family income	$21,221

Educational attainment

Percent high school graduate or higher	54.1
Percent bachelor's degree or higher	6.4

Braxton County

Bulltown Historical Area includes Saint Michael's Roman Catholic Church (foreground), built in 1978 and relocated to this site, and the nineteenth-century Cunningham-Skinner farm where Civil War troops camped and where a section of the Weston and Gauley Bridge Turnpike is located. (David R. Creel, WVU Photographic Services)

Braxton County is located at the geographic center of the state. The surface of the county is hilly, with elevations ranging from 760 to over 2,000 feet. The county is drained by the Elk, Little Kanawha, Holly, and Birch rivers. The first known permanent settlers in the territory which now embraces Braxton County were the Carpenter family, who settled at the mouth of the Holly River about 1789. The early immigrants to the area were principally from Pendleton, Randolph, and Greenbrier counties. The rugged terrain limited settlement, however, and there were few permanent settlers in Braxton County until after the turn of the century.

Braxton County was created in 1836 from parts of Kanawha, Lewis, and Nicholas counties. It was named for Carter Braxton (1736-1797), the Virginia statesman and a signer of the Declaration of Independence. The population of the county in 1840 was 2,578. The lumber, gas, and oil resources of Braxton County were exploited soon after the completion of a railway transportation network in the 1890's and 1900's. Along with the economic growth brought on by these industries came a population boom in the period from 1880 to 1910, during which population increased from 9,787 to 23,023. Population remained near this 1910 level until 1950, when it began to decline precipitously. By 1970 it had dropped to 12,666. Since then improved transportation and the development of recreation-related facilities have combined to increase both population and prosperity.

Today, Braxton County is a major center for outdoor recreation. Sutton Reservoir on the Elk River offers excellent opportunities for boating, fishing, and other recreational activities. The county is the home of the Elk River Public Hunting Area. The county's extensive forest lands and water resources have encouraged vacation activity, and numerous vacation homes have been built.

Sutton, the county seat, was originally called Newville. The town was established in 1826 and named for its founder, John D. Sutton. In 1920 it had a population of 947; in 1980 it had grown to a town of 1,192, but by 1990 had dipped back to 939.

Bulltown, located on the Little Kanawha, was named for Captain Bull, a Delaware Indian chief. He and his followers were massacred by frontiersmen in 1773. Bulltown was the site of a minor battle during the Civil War (October 12, 1863). Though Bulltown no longer exists as a community, the battle site is preserved as part of the Burnsville Reservoir Project.

Gassaway, located on the Elk River, was named for Senator Henry Gassaway Davis. It was created as a division point on the West Virginia Coal and Coke Railway between

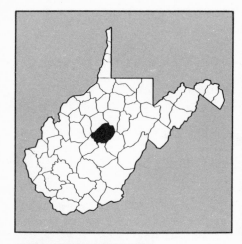

ECONOMIC PROFILE

Poverty status	
(all persons)	25.8%
65 and older	27.6%
Farms/value of farm products sold	318/$1.91 million
Retail sales	$83.72 million
Home ownership	77.5%
Value added by mining	$52.7 million
Median home value	$39,300
Median rent	$175/mo.

Elkins and Charleston and incorporated in 1904. In 1920 it had a population of 1,518; in 1990 its population was 946.

Braxton County Notables

Admiral Chester R. Bender (1914 - 1996).Commandant, US Coast Guard.

George Cogar (1930-1981). Multimillionaire founder of Mohawk Data Corporation (merged with Singer Corporation). Killed in Canadian air crash, his body was never found.

Bibliography

Sutton, John Davison. *History of Braxton County and Central West Virginia*. Sutton, 1919. Reprinted: Parsons, McClain Printing Co., 1967.

Writers' Program. West Virginia. *The Bulltown Country*. Charleston, 1940. (Folk Studies, no. 10).

Writers' Program. West Virginia. *Gassaway and Community*. [n.p.] 1942. (Folk Studies, no. 15).

Writers' Program. West Virginia. *Sutton-On-The-Elk*. Charleston, 1941. (Folk Studies, no. 123).

BRAXTON COUNTY

Land in square miles	513
Total population	12,998
Percentage rural	100
Percentage female population	51.5
Percentage African-American population	0.4
Median age	36.4
Birth rate per 1,000 pop.	14.7
Percentage 65 and older	17.1
Median family income	$20,365
Educational attainment	
Percent high school graduate or higher	56.8
Percent bachelor's degree or higher	8.1

Brooke County

Old Main at Bethany College, oldest degree-granting institution of higher education in West Virginia. Founded in 1840 by Alexander Campbell of the Christian Church (Disciples of Christ). (Bethany College)

Brooke County, in the Northern Panhandle, is one of West Virginia's smallest counties. It was created in 1797 from part of Ohio County and named in honor of Robert Brooke, Governor of Virginia from 1794 to 1796. The area had been settled for many years before the establishment of the county. The Census of 1800 gives the population of the county at 4,706.

In 1848 the General Assembly of Virginia created Hancock County from a part of Brooke County, thereby reducing Brooke's land area by almost half. In spite of this surgery, the population grew steadily, from 7,219 in 1900 to over 31,000 in 1980. This growth was made possible by an expanding industrial base. In addition to steel and other manufacturing concerns, the county has long had a significant coal industry. Coal production was slightly over one million tons in 1982.

Wellsburg, the county seat, was chartered as Charlestown in 1791. It was apparently named for Charles Prather. In 1816 the name was changed to Wellsburg, in honor of Prather's son-in-law, Alexander Wells. The first Grimes Golden apple tree is said to have stood about two miles east of Wellsburg. In 1990, the city had a population of 3,385.

Bethany, founded in 1818, is the site of Bethany College. The College was founded in 1840 by Alexander Campbell, who provided land and funds for the first building and served as first president. Bethany has remained a four-year private liberal arts college affiliated with the Christian Church (Disciples of Christ). The college is highly regarded and attracts students from throughout the country. Enrollment is approximately 800.

Brooke County Notables

Glenn "Jeep" Davis (1934-). World record hurdler who won gold medals in the 1956 and 1960 Olympics.

Joseph Doddridge (1769-1826). Clergyman, physician, and historian.

Isaac H. Duval (1824-1902). U.S. Army General in the Mexican and Civil Wars. United States Congressman 1869-1871.

Joe Funk (1917-). Retired bank executive and developer of unique "bookcase biography" depicting a person's (or corporation's) life history through the book titles. Examples were for Bing Crosby, Bill Mazeroski, Bethany College, and Grumman Aerospace. He and Dorothy have a beautiful Wellsburg estate.

Robert "Bob" Gain (1929-). All-state in football at Weirton High School, All-American at the University of Kentucky, all-pro with the Cleveland Browns.

Perry Epler Gresham (1908-1994). Long-time President of Bethany College (1953-1972). Author, minister, and entrepreneur.

Ira E. "Rat" Rogers (1895-1980). Hall of Fame football star at WVU.

Ernest Weir (1875-1957). Business leader who founded Weirton Steel Corporation.

Bibliography

Caldwell, Nancy Lee. *A History of Brooke County.* Wellsburg, Brooke County Historical Society, 1975.

Newton, J. H., G. G. Nichols, and A. G. Sprankle. *History of the Panhandle: Being Historical Collections of the Counties of Ohio, Brooke, Marshall, and Hancock, West Virginia.* Wheeling, J. A. Caldwell, 1879. Reprinted: Evansville, Ind., Unigraphic, Inc., 1973.

Brooke

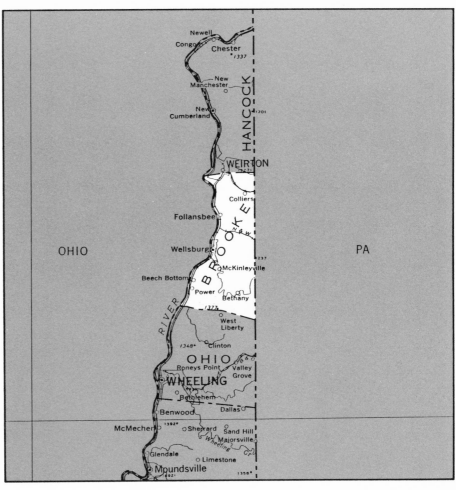

ECONOMIC PROFILE

Poverty status (all persons)	12.1%
65 and older	12.9%
Farms/value of farm products sold	79/$1.11 million
Retail sales	$93.91 million
Home ownership	79.1%
Value added by mining	NA
Median home value	$44,100
Median rent	$198/mo.

BROOKE COUNTY

Land in square miles	90
Total population	26,992
Percentage rural	45.9
Percentage female population	52.1
Percentage African-American population	0.7
Median age	37.3
Birth rate per 1,000 pop.	11.4
Percentage 65 and older	16.4
Median family income	$31,407

Educational attainment

Percent high school graduate or higher	71.6
Percent bachelor's degree or higher	12.2

Cabell County

Huntington campus of Marshall University, which was named for John Marshall, chief justice of U.S. Supreme Court from 1801 to 1835. Marshall Academy, its predecessor, was founded in 1837. (Marshall University)

Cabell County is located on the southwest border of the state and consists of broken hills and fertile river valleys. The county borders the Ohio River and is drained by its tributaries. Claim to the region was contested by both French and English, though no one knows who was the first white settler. Not until the Treaty of Paris in 1763 was the territory finally ceded to the English. In 1772, Virginia's Governor Dinwiddie made a grant of 28,628 acres to John Savage and 60 others for military service in the French and Indian War. Cabell County emerged from what was called the Savage Grant. The county was created from Kanawha County in 1809 and named in honor of William H. Cabell, Governor of Virginia from 1805 to 1808. The Census of 1810 reported a population of 2,717.

Fertile bottom land and access to the Ohio River, a main artery of commerce, made the area prosperous. Population grew steadily, reaching 13,744 by 1880. However, the real growth of the county occurred after 1900, as it developed as a transportation, commercial, and industrial center. The opening of the southeastern West Virginia coal fields in the first decade of this century made the county a major center for banking, transportation, and other services required by a rapidly growing coal industry. However, the county has never been entirely dependent on coal-related activities. The excellent transportation facilities attracted a number of industrial concerns, which have provided the county with a well-diversified economy. Taking advantage of the abundant natural gas, William Blenko developed a world-renowned glass plant in Milton. The rapidly expanding economic opportunities caused a sharp increase in population—from 29,252 in 1900 to over 108,000 fifty years later.

Cabell County has experienced many changes in the location of its county seat. Guyandotte was county seat from 1809 to 1814 when the seat was moved to Barboursville. It returned to Guyandotte in 1863 because of "marauding incursions of rebels." It was returned to Barboursville after the war, only to be moved in 1887 to Huntington where it has remained.

Huntington, formerly known as Holderby's Landing, was incorporated in 1871. It was named for Collis P. Huntington, the president of the Chesapeake and Ohio Railroad. Huntington was selected the site of the western terminus of the railroad. An engineer employed by the railroad laid out a large city with wide streets, making Huntington the only planned city in the state. The city, which had a population of 3,174 in 1880, grew rapidly, and in 1980 had a population of over 63,000. However, this dropped to 54,844 by 1990.

Marshall University, located in Huntington, traces its origin to 1837, when Marshall Academy was organized. In 1867 the West Virginia Legislature created the State Normal School at Marshall College. The college weathered many lean years, but began to grow steadily after 1900. Marshall was granted university status in 1961, and a School of Medicine was established in 1974. The enrollment is approximately 11,000. Marshall's Thundering Herd football team won national Division 1-AA titles (moved to Div. 1 in 1997).

Cabell County Notables

William Campbell (1923-   ). U.S. amateur golf champion.

Harold Greer (1937-   ). Marshall University and National Basketball Association all-pro player.

Ken Hechler (1914-   ). U.S. Congressman from 1959 to 1977; author of *The Bridge at Remagen* and *Working With Truman.* Currently Secretary of State of West Virginia.

Dwight W. Morrow (1873-1931). U.S. Ambassador; father of Anne Morrow Lindbergh.

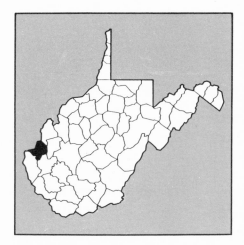

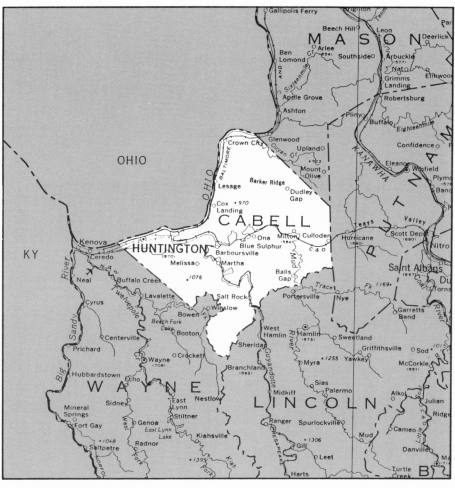

ECONOMIC PROFILE

Poverty status	
(all persons)	19.1%
65 and older	14.7%
Farms/value of farm products sold	375/$1.96 million
Retail sales	$799.64 million
Home ownership	64.7%
Value added by mining	NA
Median home value	$52,800
Median rent	$241/mo.

Milton "Soupy" Sales (Supman) (1926-   ). Nationally famous comedian.

Alex Schoenbaum (1915-1996). Multimillionaire philanthropist and restauranteur (Shoney's Inc., with 1800 restaurants).

Dr. Carter Godwin Woodson (1875-1950). Black educator and historian.

Bibliography

"Hardesty's Cabell County." *West Virginia Heritage Encyclopedia.* Supplemental Series, vol. 6.

Miller, Doris C. *A Centennial History of Huntington,* W. Va. 1871-1971. Huntington, Huntington Centennial Commission, 1971.

CABELL COUNTY

Land in square miles	282
Total population	96,827
Percentage rural	27.9
Percentage female population	53.2
Percentage African-American population	4.1
Median age	35.8
Birth rate per 1,000 pop.	12.3
Percentage 65 and older	16.4
Median family income	$28,090

Educational attainment

Percent high school graduate or higher	71.9
Percent bachelor's degree or higher	18.9

Calhoun County

Above: Donkey engine, a fixture at the annual Molasses Festival atArnoldsburg, operates the crushers that squeeze the juice out of the sorghum stalks. (Merrill Pollack, The Calhoun Chronicle)

Right: (L. Victor Haines, WVU Photographic Services)

Calhoun County is located in the west-central part of West Virginia. Most of the county is drained by the Little Kanawha River and its tributaries. The first permanent settlement in the area was about 1810 near present-day Arnoldsburg. Calhoun County was created in 1856 from Gilmer County and named for John C. Calhoun of South Carolina. The county was thinly populated, with a population of only 2,502 in 1860.

Calhoun County long remained isolated and relatively poor. There were no towns of any size, and the vast majority of the population depended on farming and grazing of livestock. The production of oil and gas began to assume importance starting shortly before the turn of the century. While oil and gas development brought much needed money into the area, it did not, and still does not, provide a large number of steady, full-time jobs.

Thus, the county's population has remained relatively small. It peaked at 12,455 in 1940 and declined steadily to slightly over 7,000 in 1970. The introduction of some light industries caused the population to increase in recent years to 7,885 in 1990.

Calhoun is in the heart of West Virginia's "country roads" area. The Little Kanawha River and tributaries provide recreational opportunities, including excellent muskie fishing. Dams along the Little Kanawha at Burnsville, Steer Creek, and West Fork provide flood control and help make a vacationland of the area. However, the devastating floods of March 1997 hit Calhoun County and claimed the life of 73-year-old Kenneth Harris of Stumptown. The grave of Mike Fink, the famous riverboater, is in this county south of Arnoldsburg.

Grantsville, situated on the Little Kanawha River, is the county seat. It was named for General U. S. Grant. Calhoun County, like many others, found it difficult to agree upon the location of the courthouse. Sectional rivalries were keen, and it was not until about 1870 that the courthouse was built in Grantsville. Prior to this, Arnoldsburg, Bigbend, Brooksville, and Pine Creek were the county seats. The population of Grantsville in 1980 was 788; in 1990 it was 671.

Calhoun County Notables
John M. Hamilton (1855-1916). Congressman and member of the House of Delegates.

Robert H. Mollohan (1909-   )
Alan B. Mollohan (1943-   ). Members US House of Representatives, (Father and son).

Boyd Stutler (1889-1970). Journalist, soldier, and historian.

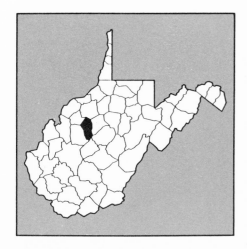

ECONOMIC PROFILE

Poverty status (all persons)	32.0%
65 and older	35.2%
Farms/value of farm products sold	158/$668,000
Retail sales	$17.31 million
Home ownership	76.7%
Value added by mining	NA
Median home value	$33,200
Median rent	$145/mo.

John Marshall Wolverton (1872-1944). Born in Bigbend, he served two terms in the US House of Representatives, 1925-27 and 1929-31.

Bibliography

Calhoun County Centennial Corp. *Calhoun County Centennial, 1856-1956.* Grantsville, 1956.

"Hardesty's Calhoun County." *West Virginia Heritage Encyclopedia.* Supplemental Series, vol. 3.

Knotts, Robert J., Jr. and Robert E. Stevens. *Calhoun County in the Civil War.* Grantsville, Calhoun County Historical and Genealogical Society, 1982.

CALHOUN COUNTY

Land in square miles	280
Total population	7,885
Percentage rural	100
Percentage female population	50.9
Percentage African-American population	0.0
Median age	35.6
Birth rate per 1,000 pop.	12.0
Percentage 65 and older	15.8
Median family income	$17,671

Educational attainment

Percent high school graduate or higher	56.3
Percent bachelor's degree or higher	6.8

Clay County

Above: Golden Delicious Apple, one of the most important varieties in the world, was discovered on Porters Creek in 1914. Stark Brothers Nurseries and Orchards in Missouri, which purchased the tree, estimates that more than 24 million Golden Delicious trees have sprung from the original tree. (R. Ferrell Friend)

Right: Float fishing on the Elk River. (R. Ferrell Friend)

Clay County is situated in the central part of the state and is drained by the Elk River and its tributaries. The county was formed in 1858 from parts of Braxton and Nicholas counties and named in honor of Henry Clay. The rugged terrain and lack of transportation made the area relatively unattractive to settlers. The population was 1,787 in 1860 and grew slowly to 4,659 thirty years later. The county began to experience substantial increases in both population and prosperity in the 1890's as the construction of what was to become the Coal & Coke Railroad opened up the area. Several companies, the largest of which was the Elk River Coal and Lumber Company, began to establish major coal and timber operations.

Coal mining, which became centered about Widen, grew increasingly important. Production, only 36,000 tons in 1910, grew to over 400,000 tons in 1920 and 800,000 tons by 1960. However, the closing of the Widen operations in the early 1960's caused a sharp decline in production. In 1983 coal production was 120,000 tons, over half surface mined. The decline in mining employment resulted in a loss of population, which went from 15,206 in 1940 to 9,330 in 1970. However, population increased to 11,265 by 1980, with many residents finding employment in the nearby Kanawha Valley. The area's great natural beauty has attracted an increasing number of summer residents. Full-time residential population in 1990, however, was just under 10,000.

Flints, arrowheads, and bones found at Bone Town Gap indicate the area was once an Indian hunting ground; it was also used by early white settlers as a hunting preserve.

Clay, the county seat, was incorporated in 1895. It was formerly known as Henry and Clay Court House. The population in 1980 was 940; in 1990 it was 592. The famous Golden Delicious Apple was developed near here.

Clay County Notables
Ed L. Boggs (1869-1952). Member of House of Delegates, as were his father James M. and grandfather James A.

Lloyd Harman Elliot (1918-   ). Leading educator who became President of the University of Maine, 1958-1965, and George Washington University, 1965-1980s.

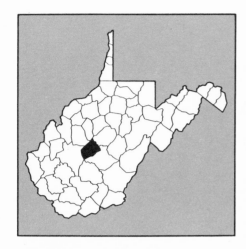

ECONOMIC PROFILE

Poverty status (all persons)	39.2%
65 and older	33.7%
Farms/value of farm products sold	97/$440,000
Retail sales	$15.66 million
Home ownership	76.0%
Value added by mining	NA
Median home value	$33,000
Median rent	$140/mo.

Bibliography

Byrne, William E. R. *Tale of the Elk*. Charleston, West Virginia Publishing Co., 1940. 455 pp.

Clay County High School. *Hickory & Lady Slippers: Life and Legend of Clay County People,* vol. 1. Clay, 1977.

CLAY COUNTY

Land in square miles	346
Total population	9,983
Percentage rural	100
Percentage female population	50.7
Percentage African-American population	0.0
Median age	32.9
Birth rate per 1,000 pop.	14.4
Percentage 65 and older	12.8
Median family income	$16,130

Educational attainment

Percent high school graduate or higher	49.4
Percent bachelor's degree or higher	6.2

Doddridge County

Doddridge County Courthouse at West Union. (L. Victor Haines, WVU Photographic Services)

Doddridge County was formed in 1845 from parts of Harrison, Tyler, Ritchie, and Lewis counties. It was named in honor of Phillip Doddridge (1772-1832), a United States congressman and Virginia state legislator. The terrain of the county is hilly, with only a small amount of level land along streams and creeks. The land is drained primarily by Middle Island Creek, so named from Middle Island on the Ohio River near the creek's mouth. This stream has been called the "longest creek in the world" and is 75.3 miles long. Doddridge County was first settled about 1800, and by 1850 it had a population of approximately 8,000.

The completion of the Baltimore and Ohio Railroad through the county in 1857 brought about the beginning of production of cross-ties for the ex-panding railroads, was the county's first industry. The most lucrative industry, however, has always been the extraction of oil and natural gas. Though drilling started in the county in the 1880's, it was not until 1892 that the oil boom began. The Crash of 1929 brought an end to the oil and gas boom, but there was a resurgence of this industry in the 1960's, and drilling continues today. The major industries are oil and gas production, lumbering, and farming. The population of Doddridge County in 1900 was 13,689. From this peak, the population declined to 6,389 in 1970, but has increased recently.

West Union, the county seat, was first settled about 1807 by the Davis family. Known as Lewisport or Union until the completion of the railroad station in 1857, West Union was incorporated in 1881, and in 1990 had a population of 830.

Doddridge County Notables

Joseph H. Diss Debar (1820-1905). Designer of the State Seal, Commissioner of Immigration for West Virginia, and leader in the statehood movement.

Corma A. Mowrey (1910 - 1990). Country school teacher (born in Big Isaac) who became president of the National Education Association.

Matthew M. Neely (1874-1958). Born in Grove, he served three separate terms as US Senator from West Virginia (1923-29, 1931-41, and 1949-58), and was Governor of West Virginia, 1941-45.

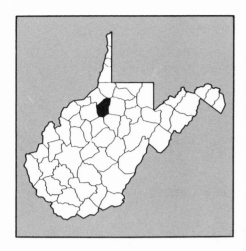

ECONOMIC PROFILE

Poverty status (all persons)	23.0%
65 and older	21.3%
Farms/value of farm products sold	272/$903,000
Retail sales	$5.99 million
Home ownership	82.4%
Value added by mining	NA
Median home value	$33,800
Median rent	$157/mo.

Bibliography

Doddridge County Historical Society. *The History of Doddridge County, West Virginia, 1979: A Collection of Historical Sketches, Church and Family Histories. 1979.*

"Hardesty's Doddridge County." *West Virginia Heritage Encyclopedia.* Supplemental Series, vol. 2.

DODDRIDGE COUNTY

Land in square miles	321
Total population	6,994
Percentage rural	100
Percentage female population	50.5
Percentage African-American population	0.0
Median age	35.4
Birth rate per 1,000 pop.	12.0
Percentage 65 and older	16.2
Median family income	$19,830

Educational attainment

Percent high school graduate or higher	64.6
Percent bachelor's degree or higher	10.3

Fayette County

Above: New River Gorge Bridge on U.S. 19, which is 1,700 feet long–longest steel arch bridge in the world. (L. Victor Haines, WVU Photographic Services)

Right: View from Hawks Nest State Park in Fayette County. (West Virginia Department of Commerce)

Fayette County is situated in the southern tier of counties. The area is mountainous and is drained by the New and Gauley rivers. Fayette County was created in 1831 from parts of Greenbrier, Kanawha, Nicholas, and Logan counties and was named in honor of the Marquis de Lafayette. The population was for many years both scant and scattered. A rugged terrain and lack of transportation did not encourage inmigration, nor did the extremely unsettled conditions during the Civil War. The county remained poor, and the population was less than 7,000 in 1870.

Fayette County had long been known to be rich in coal, but the lack of transportation made development impossible. However, in 1872-73 the Chesapeake and Ohio Railroad reached the area and opened up the New River and Kanawha coal fields. In 1873 Joseph L. Beury started to ship coal from his newly opened mine at Quinnimont. From that date, mine after mine opened and coal production increased at a phenomenal rate. Coal production reached 1.5 million tons in 1888 and 4.5 million in 1900. Fayette County was the largest coal producer in the state until overtaken by McDowell County in 1905. Production peaked in 1940 (12.4 million tons) and has declined more or less steadily since. Population has tended to parallel coal production, growing rapidly from 11,560 in 1880 to 51,903 in 1910. Population peaked in 1950 (82,443) and declined to a low of 47,952 in 1990, but has started to grow again recently.

Fayette County includes the New River Gorge, which is rapidly becoming an important recreational area. Whitewater rafting, the spectacular suspension bridge, and the old coal mining towns attract an increasing number of visitors. The National Park Service is developing parts of the gorge as a National River.

Fayetteville, the county seat, was first called Vandalia, after Abraham Vandal who acquired the site about 1818. The town was incorporated in 1883 and renamed Fayetteville. Its population in 1990 was 2,182. Other important towns include Montgomery, Mount Hope, and Oak Hill. At Montgomery is West Virginia University Institute of Technology, a state-supported school established in 1895 as a preparatory branch of West Virginia University. After several changes in name and function, it assumed its present name in 1996. The school has over 3,000 students.

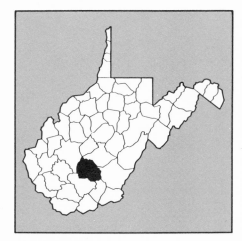

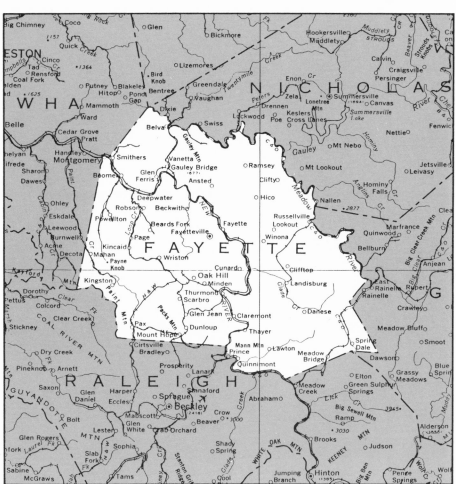

ECONOMIC PROFILE

Poverty status	
(all persons)	24.4%
65 and older	15.3%
Farms/value of farm products sold	185/$1.27 million
Retail sales	$197.72 million
Home ownership	76.4%
Value added by mining	$60.2 million
Median home value	$34,500
Median rent	$180/mo.

Fayette County Notables

John F. "Sheriff" Blake (1899-1976). Major league pitcher for eleven years.

George Cafego (1915-   ). All-state quarterback at Oak Hill High School, All-American at U. of Tennessee.

William R. Laird III (1917-1974). Served as US Senator in 1956.

Admiral T. Joseph Lopez (1940-   ). Appointed Commander of US Navy Sixth Fleet in 1992, and USN-Europe in 1996.

Okey L. Patteson (1898-1989). Governor of West Virginia, 1949-1953.

Edgar "Tut" Tutweiler (1919-   ). Golfer who won the State amateur title eleven times.

Bibliography

Peters, J. T. and H. B. Carden. *History of Fayette County, West Virginia.* Charleston, 1926. Reprinted: Parsons, McClain Printing Co., 1972.

Tams, W. P., Jr. *The Smokeless Coal Fields of West Virginia: A Brief History.* Morgantown, West Virginia University Press, 1963.

FAYETTE COUNTY

Land in square miles	667
Total population	47,952
Percentage rural	85.8
Percentage female population	52.1
Percentage African-American population	6.3
Median age	36.2
Birth rate per 1,000 pop.	11.8
Percentage 65 and older	17.1
Median family income	$20,848

Educational attainment

Percent high school graduate or higher	57.1
Percent bachelor's degree or higher	8.8

Gilmer County

Cedar Creek State Park near Glenville features this fishing lake, as well as a swimming pool and tennis. (L. Victor Haines, WVU Photographic Services)

Gilmer County is located in the central part of the state and lies within the drainage basin of the Little Kanawha River. The county was created in 1845 from parts of Lewis and Kanawha counties and named for Thomas W. Gilmer (1802-1844), a governor of Virginia. In 1856 the western portions of the county were detached to form Calhoun County. In 1860, on the eve of the Civil War, the population of Gilmer County was 3,759. During the war, North-South sympathies were about equally divided, with 360 men entering the Federal Army and an approximately equal number joining the Southern forces.

Gilmer County's economy was for many years based almost entirely on agriculture and lumbering. The economic base was widened in the 1890's with the development of the oil and gas fields. Coal mining began to be-come important about 1908, and by 1915 production had reached 137,000 tons. Coal production peaked in 1964 at 1,223,942 tons but declined rapidly thereafter and is no longer of great significance. New drilling technology has given renewed life to the oil and gas industry and it is now a major source of income. Gilmer County's population reached a peak of 12,046 in 1940.

Dekalb was the first county seat. Job's Church, a hand-hewn log church begun in 1860, is a historical landmark here.

Glenville, the county seat, is located on the Little Kanawha River. When laid out in 1845, the town was called Hartford. By an act of the Virginia Legislature in 1856, it was renamed Glenville because of the glen or valley in which it was located. The population of the town was 327 in 1920; in 1990 it was 1,922. Glenville State College, estab-lished by an act of the State Legislature in 1872, is a state-supported, co-educational institution of higher learning. The college has an enrollment of over 2,300. The West Virginia Folk Festival is held annually in Glenville.

Gilmer County Notables

Dr. Dana L. Farnsworth (1905-1986). Commander US Navy Medical Corps, 1941-1945; Chairman, first International Conference on Student Health, 1956.

Patrick W. Gainer (1903-1981). Leading authority on Appalachian folklore and music.

John (1874-1951) and Maude E. Kee. Husband and wife who served in US House of Representatives (he from 1933-51; she, 1951-65).

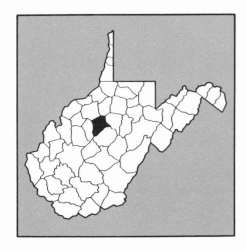

ECONOMIC PROFILE

Poverty status (all persons)	33.5%
65 and older	36.1%
Farms/value of farm products sold	237/$1.51 million
Retail sales	$17.05 million
Home ownership	71.4%
Value added by mining	NA
Median home value	$42,100
Median rent	$193/mo.

Joseph E. Miller (1935-   ). All-state basketball star at Sand Fork High School, national record-setter at Alderson Broaddus College (NAIA All-American).

Bibliography

Gilmer County Historical Society. *Bicentennial Biographies, Gilmer County, West Virginia.* Glenville, 1976.

"Hardesty's Gilmer County." *West Virginia Heritage Encyclopedia.* Supplemental Series, vol. 7.

GILMER COUNTY

Land in square miles	340
Total population	7,669
Percentage rural	100
Percentage female population	50.4
Percentage African-American population	0.4
Median age	33.2
Birth rate per 1,000 pop.	10.0
Percentage 65 and older	16.3
Median family income	$16,994

Educational attainment

Percent high school graduate or higher	56.6
Percent bachelor's degree or higher	14.2

Grant County

Above: Fairfax Stone marks the boundary between Maryland and West Virginia as determined by the U.S. Supreme Court after a dispute between the two states. (L. Victor Haines, WVU Photographic Services)

Right: Coal-burning, electric-generating plant of Virginia Electric and Power Company at Mount Storm. West Virginia is the major exporter of electricity in the nation. (Governor's Office of Economic and Community Development)

Grant County is located in the Eastern Panhandle of the state in what was once called the Northern Neck of Virginia. It is a mountainous area, though it includes broad flat valleys along the major streams. The land is drained by the Potomac River and its tributaries. Drawn by the rich limestone soil along the rivers, white settlers came early to the area. In 1754 Fort George, named for George Washington who surveyed in the area, was built on the South Branch near Petersburg. Also in 1754, Hampshire County, which then included present-day Grant County, was formed. In 1786, the western part of Hampshire County was annexed to form Hardy County.

During the Civil War, the area now known as Grant County was a borderland between North and South. In 1866 the West Virginia Legislature created Grant County, naming it for Ulysses S. Grant, and separating it from Hardy County. Grant County began to prosper after the war. A spur of the B & O Railroad was built, connecting Petersburg with Romney and the main line of the B & O in Hampshire County. Timber and agricultural products were produced for market. In 1870 the population was 4,467.

In 1903 the first coal mines were opened in the eastern part of the county, producing 31,908 tons that year. Though coal production has varied tremendously over the years—the mines all but shut down between 1932 and 1940—the industry remains a major one in the county. In 1980 the county produced over 2.4 million tons. Agriculture is the most important industry, accounting for over one-quarter of the county's employment, and producing poultry, hay and grain, livestock, timber, fruit, and maple sugar. The population of Grant County has increased from approximately 4,000 at the time of its establishment to 8,993 in 1920 and to 10,428 in 1990.

Several recreational areas are located in the county, including Monongahela National Forest and Smoke Hole Caverns. The most popular recreational activities are hunting, fishing, and whitewater rafting on the South Branch. The tourist industry has become an increasingly important part of the local economy. An example of the area's rustic but rewarding accommodations is Smoke Hole Lodge (near Petersburg), run by West Virginians – the Stifels – since the 1930s.

Petersburg, the county seat, was named for Jacob Peters, a landowner who settled in the area in 1746 and operated a general store. The town is located on the South Branch at the mouth of Lunice Creek and was in-

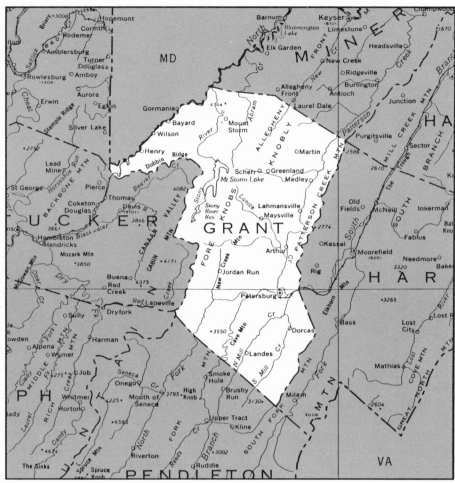

ECONOMIC PROFILE

Poverty status	
(all persons)	15.5%
65 and older	25.7%
Farms/value of farm products sold	353/$14.41 million
Retail sales	$33.75 million
Home ownership	81.5%
Value added by mining	NA
Median home value	$49,900
Median rent	$178/mo.

corporated in 1910. In 1920 it was a small farming town of 834; by 1990 it had grown to 2,360.

Grant County Notables

Frank H. Babb (1900-1970). President of the American Red Cross during World War II.

George S. VanMeter (1844-1922). Civil War veteran, served in the House of Delegates.

Bibliography

Judy, Elvin L. *History of Grant and Hardy Counties, West Virginia.* Charleston, Charleston Printing Co., 1951.

Stallings, James L., Sharon Lord, and Nelson L. Bills. *Resources of the Upper South Branch Valley, West Virginia.* West Virginia University Agricultural Experiment Station Bulletin 551. Morgantown, 1967.

GRANT COUNTY

Land in square miles	480
Total population	10,428
Percentage rural	100
Percentage female population	50.8
Percentage African-American population	1.0
Median age	35.7
Birth rate per 1,000 pop.	12.3
Percentage 65 and older	14.8
Median family income	$25,327

Educational attainment

Percent high school graduate or higher	60.2
Percent bachelor's degree or higher	8.6

Greenbrier County

Old Stone Church in Lewisburg has been in continuous use since it was built in 1796. The Presbyterian Church contains what used to be a gallery where slaves worshipped. Civil War soldiers are buried in the adjoining cemetery. (West Virginia Department of Commerce)

Greenbrier County is located in the southeastern part of the state. The terrain is mountainous, but there is ample level and gently sloping land. The area is drained by the Greenbrier, Meadow, and Cherry rivers and their tributaries. Greenbrier is the second largest county in area in the state. The first known white settlements were made in the 1750's, and by 1755 there were enough settlers in the Greenbrier area to justify the construction of Fort Savannah at the site of present-day Lewisburg. In 1767 the Cherokee and Iroquois tribes surrendered their rights to this area and the land was opened to white settlement. Greenbrier County was formed from parts of Montgomery and Botetourt (Virginia) counties in 1778 and named for the Greenbrier River. In 1790 it had a population of 6,015.

There are several mineral springs located in Greenbrier County which were visited by those seeking cures from various ailments. In 1809 a hotel was built at White Sulphur Springs and the spring became a popular tourist attraction. In 1811 operations commenced at Blue Sulphur Springs. By the 1830's the White and Blue were summer gathering places for the elite of Southern society. The resort at Blue Sulphur was abandoned in the 1850's and burned by Northern troops in the Civil War, but the White Sulphur establishment continued to operate after the war and has become an internationally known resort.

With the completion of the Chesapeake and Ohio Railroad through the county in 1873, the development of the region's timber and coal reserves began. Logs were cut along the Greenbrier River and floated downstream to Ronceverte. In 1909 the Meadow River Company began operations along the Meadow River and founded the town of Rainelle. From 1910 to 1970 the Meadow River Mill was said to be the largest sawmilling operation in the world. Coal was mined in Greenbrier County as early as 1840, but the commercial exploitation of the high-quality, low-sulphur coal did not begin until after World War I. Production peaked in 1950 at 2,046,535 tons, but has since declined.

The population of the county has expanded and contracted in response to economic activity. From 1880 to 1930, the population more than doubled, increasing from 15,060 in 1880 to 35,878 in 1930. Population peaked in 1950 at 39,295, but by 1970 it had dropped to 32,090. However, there has been a significant increase during the past ten years, to about 35,000 in 1990.

Lewisburg, the county seat, is the third oldest town in the state. It was first called Savannah for the fort built here in 1755; it was later called Big Levels and Camp Union. The town was chartered in 1774 and named in honor of General Andrew Lewis, who defeated Cornstalk and his Shawnee warriors at the Battle of Point Pleasant. There are many gracious homes and historic sites in the town, including the Old Stone Church, which was built in 1796 and is the oldest Presbyterian Church west of the Allegheny Mountains still in use. Lewisburg had a population of 3,598 in 1990.

White Sulphur Springs. Named for the clear sulphur springs in the area. The springs attracted many visitors, and White Sulphur Springs was a well known spa by the middle of the last century. Located in the town is the Greenbrier Hotel, a world-famous resort.

Greenbrier County Notables

Major General John L. Hines (1868-1946). U.S. Army Chief of Staff, 1924-1926.

Homer A. Holt (1898-1975). Governor of West Virginia, 1937-1941.

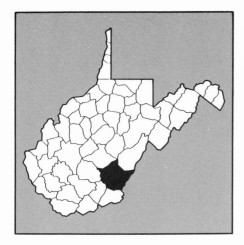

ECONOMIC PROFILE

Poverty status	
(all persons)	17.9%
65 and older	20.0%
Farms/value of farm products sold	729/$13.89 million
Retail sales	$180.85 million
Home ownership	75.6%
Value added by mining	$33.2 million
Median home value	$44,000
Median rent	$192/mo.

Henry M. Matthews (1834-1884). Governor of West Virginia, 1877-1881.

Margaret Prescott Montague (1878-1955). Novelist and poet.

Percival Reniers (1894-1992). Professor and author, *The Springs of Virginia,* etc.

Joseph Rosier (1870-1951). US Senator from West Virginia, 1941-42.

Samuel J. Snead (1912-). Golfer long associated with the Greenbrier Hotel.

Bibliography

Dayton, Ruth Woods. *Greenbrier Pioneers and Their Homes.* Charleston, West Virginia Publishing Co., 1942. Reprinted: Charleston, Education Foundation, Inc., 1957.

Dayton, Ruth Woods. *Lewisburg Landmarks.* Charleston, Education Foundation, Inc., 1957.

Greenbrier County Bicentennial Committee. *Greenbrier County Bicentennial 1778-1978.* Lewisburg, 1978.

GREENBRIER COUNTY

Land in square miles	1,025
Total population	34,693
Percentage rural	81.6
Percentage female population	52.1
Percentage African-American population	3.7
Median age	37.3
Birth rate per 1,000 pop.	11.4
Percentage 65 and older	16.9
Median family income	$23,819

Educational attainment

Percent high school graduate or higher	63.0
Percent bachelor's degree or higher	11.5

Hampshire County

Above: Oldest building in Romney is the Wilson-Woodrow-Mytinger House, built about 1770. (Phillip R. Pitts)

Right: Literary Hall in Romney, built in 1870, where the Literary Society staged debates. (West Virginia Department of Culture and History)

Hampshire County, the oldest county in the state, lies in the Eastern Panhandle and is one of the counties comprising what was once known as the Northern Neck of Virginia. The land is mostly mountainous, although it includes broad flat valleys along the major streams. The land is wholly within the drainage basin of the Potomac River. Its principal watercourses are the North and South Branches of the Potomac, the Great Cacapon River, and Mill Creek. In the early days, many Indians passed through the South Branch Valley along the Seneca Trail, the most important north-south Indian trail in the state.

The white man came into the area now called Hampshire County in about 1725, when John Van Meter and other Indian traders and hunters came to the valleys. By 1740 white settlers had established themselves along the South Branch. The rich bottom land was settled quickly, and in 1754 Hampshire County was formed from parts of Frederick and Augusta (Virginia) counties. It included what is now Hampshire, Hardy, Grant, Mineral, and part of Morgan counties.

During the Civil War the county was pro-Southern, though there was considerable pro-Northern sentiment in the western part of the county (which would in 1866 become Mineral County). Though no major battles were fought in the county, it was never free of soldiers. With the B & O Railroad running along the county's northern border, control of this area was critical to both sides. Romney, which was strategically located on the Northwest Turnpike (now U.S. 50), was the focus of many skirmishes, changing hands 56 times.

Hampshire County has always been a predominantly agricultural county noted for its livestock and orchards. The population remained remarkably constant over the years, remaining at approximately 11,700 from 1900 to 1970. However, the 1980 and 1990 Censuses showed a significant increase.

Romney, the county seat, was established by Lord Fairfax in 1762 and is the oldest county seat and one of the oldest incorporated towns in the state. It was named after a port city in England. In 1810 the town had a population of 217 whites, 77 slaves, and one freedman. In 1900 its population was 580 and 1,966 in 1990. The West Virginia Schools for the Deaf and Blind are located in Romney.

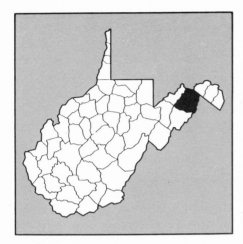

ECONOMIC PROFILE

Poverty status (all persons)	18.2%
65 and older	27.6%
Farms/value of farm products sold	492/$10.31 million
Retail sales	$40.66 million
Home ownership	81.1%
Value added by mining	NA
Median home value	$50,500
Median rent	$179/mo.

Hampshire County Notables

John J. Cornwell (1867-1953). Governor of West Virginia, 1917-1921.

John J. Jacob (1829-1893). Governor of West Virginia, 1871-1877.

Herman G. Kump (1877-1962). Governor of West Virginia, 1933-37.

Rae Ellen McKee (1958-). National Teacher of the Year, 1991.

Bibliography

Brannon, Selden W. *Historic Hampshire.* Parsons, McClain Printing Co., 1976.

Maxwell, Hu and H. L. Swisher. *History of Hampshire County, West Virginia from its earliest settlement to the present.* Morgantown, 1897. Reprinted: Parsons, McClain Printing Co., 1972.

HAMPSHIRE COUNTY

Land in square miles	644
Total population	16,498
Percentage rural	100
Percentage female population	50.5
Percentage African-American population	0.7
Median age	34.5
Birth rate per 1,000 pop.	14.4
Percentage 65 and older	13.7
Median family income	$24,164

Educational attainment

Percent high school graduate or higher	61.8
Percent bachelor's degree or higher	9.0

Hancock County

Weirton Steel Corporation, largest employee-owned firm in the United States. (L. Victor Haines, WVU Photographic Services)

Hancock County, smallest of West Virginia's counties, is located at the northern tip of the state's Northern Panhandle. The first Europeans to visit the area were French adventurers led by Celoron de Blainville in 1749. They buried lead tablets in the hills along the Ohio River in an attempt to claim the river valley for France. However, settlers from the English colonies soon moved into the area. The earliest permanent settlement was Holliday's Cove on the southern boundary of present-day Hancock County. It was named after John Holliday, who built a log cabin there in 1776. Hancock County was formed in 1848 from Brooke County with a population of about 4,000, and named after John Hancock, first signer of the Declaration of Independence.

Near the county's (and state's) northernmost point, a monument along Route 39 just north of Chester states: " . . . the beginning for surveying the public lands of the United States. There on September 30, 1785, Thomas Hutchins, first geographer of the United States began the 'Line of the Seven Ranges.'"

Unlike many counties in West Virginia, Hancock's economy has been based not on coal mining or agriculture, but on industry. Steel has been the foundation of the county's economy. The industrial base has made for high per-capita income and concentration of population. The county's population has grown slowly over the years to an all-time high of 40,418 in 1980, although it fell to about 35,000 in 1990. Hancock County is one of the most densely populated

counties of West Virginia with over 400 persons per square mile.

New Cumberland, the county seat, is located beside the Ohio River and in 1990 had a population of 1,363. The town was laid out in 1839 by John Cuppy and was originally named Vernon. A number of early town citizens objected to this name, and by 1840 the name was changed to New Cumberland.

Weirton, the county's largest city and its economic heart, had in 1990 a population of 22,124. The city was founded in 1909 by the Weirton Steel Corporation which was owned by the Weir family. Weirton was a town built by steel, for steel. Today, the steel mills are owned and operated by the workers.

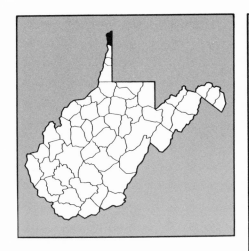

ECONOMIC PROFILE

Poverty status (all persons)	11.9%
65 and older	10.4%
Farms/value of farm products sold	86/$862,000
Retail sales	$144.59 million
Home ownership	76.7%
Value added by mining	NA
Median home value	$45,600
Median rent	$221/mo.

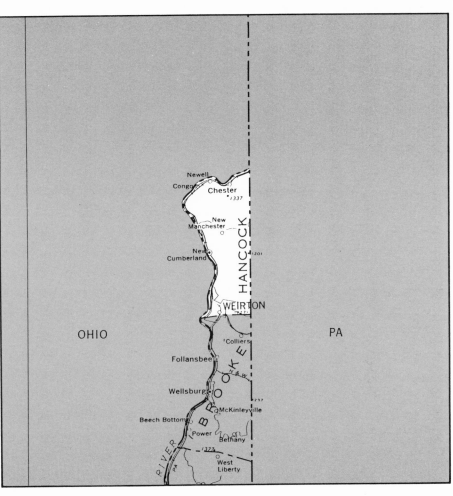

Hancock County Notables

John H. Atkinson (1820-1880). State senator and a delegate to the Wheeling Convention that established West Virginia.

John B. Hale (1831-1905). Civil War officer, became a US Congressman from Missouri.

Bibliography

Boyd, Peter. *History of Northern West Virginia Panhandle, Embracing Ohio, Marshall, Brooke, and Hancock Counties.* Topeka, Kansas, Historical Publishing Co., 1927. 2 vol.

Orler, Inez. *The History of Weirton.* New York, Carlton Press, 1977.

Welch, Jack. *History of Hancock County, Virginia and West Virginia.* Wheeling, Wheeling News Printing and Litho. Co., 1963.

HANCOCK COUNTY

Land in square miles	85
Total population	35,233
Percentage rural	39.0
Percentage female population	52.1
Percentage African-American population	2.6
Median age	37.7
Birth rate per 1,000 pop.	11.0
Percentage 65 and older	16.0
Median family income	$30,576

Educational attainment

Percent high school graduate or higher	72.5
Percent bachelor's degree or higher	8.9

Hardy County

West Virginia's poultry industry is concentrated in Hardy County. (L. Victor Haines, WVU Photographic Services)

Hardy County lies in the Eastern Panhandle of the state and is one of the counties comprising what was once known as the Northern Neck of Virginia. The land is mostly mountainous, though it includes broad flat valleys along the major streams. It is drained by three tributaries of the Potomac River—the South Branch of the Potomac, the Lost River, and the Cacapon River.

In 1748 George Washington came to the South Branch Valley and helped survey 55,000 acres for Lord Fairfax, an English nobleman who had inherited a vast tract of land in the area. Drawn by the rich limestone soil along the rivers, white settlers soon followed. In 1786 the Virginia Legislature created Hardy County from a portion of Hampshire County. It was named for Samuel Hardy, a distinguished Virginian who had served in the Continental Congress. By 1790 the population was 7,336, including 369 slaves and 411 non-white freedmen.

In 1860 the population of the county stood at 9,864, with 1,073 slaves. During the Civil War the majority of the people allied themselves with the South, though there were many Union supporters in the northwestern parts of the county. Though no major battles were fought in the county, there were many skirmishes. In 1866 the West Virginia Legislature divided the county roughly in half, creating Grant County from the northwestern, pro-Northern half. Hardy has remained a predominantly agricultural county with some of the best farmland in the state located along the South Branch. Today poultry is the single most important agricultural product, and Moorefield is known as the "Poultry Capital of West Virginia."

Hardy County has several important recreational resources. Part of the George Washington National Forest lies within the county, as does the Lost River State Park, consisting of some 3,700 acres. The South Branch boasts some of the best fishing and whitewater rafting in the East, and the tourist industry has become increasingly important.

Moorefield, the county seat, is located on the South Branch of the Potomac. It was chartered in 1744 and named for Conrad Moore, the owner of the townsite. The town has always been a shipping and trading center for this rich agricultural region. In 1920 its population was 630; in 1990 it was 2,148.

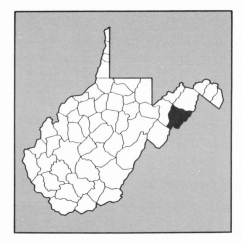

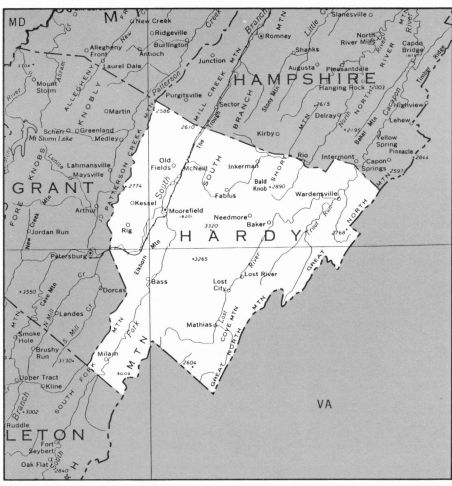

ECONOMIC PROFILE

Poverty status (all persons)	14.6%
65 and older	30.4%
Farms/value of farm products sold	460/$40.27 million
Retail sales	$32.03 million
Home ownership	82.2%
Value added by mining	NA
Median home value	$49,300
Median rent	$186/mo.

Hardy County Notables

Robert E. Lee (1807-1870). Confederate Commanding General who had a "summer cabin" at Lost River State Park, originally constructed by his father, US General Henry "Lighthorse Harry" Lee.

Willard D. VanDiver (1854-1936). Assistant Treasurer of the US and a Congressman from Missouri.

Bibliography

Judy, Elvin L. *History of Grant and Hardy Counties, West Virginia.* Charleston, Charleston Printing Co., 1951.

Moore, Alvin E. *History of Hardy County of the Borderland.* Parsons, McClain Printing Co., 1963.

Stallings, James L., Sharon Lord, and Nelson L. Bills. *Resources of the Upper South Branch Valley, West Virginia.* West Virginia University Agricultural Experiment Station Bulletin 551. Morgantown, 1967.

HARDY COUNTY

Land in square miles	585
Total population	10,977
Percentage rural	100
Percentage female population	50.7
Percentage African-American population	1.9
Median age	36.1
Birth rate per 1,000 pop.	13.6
Percentage 65 and older	15.3
Median family income	$25,843

Educational attainment

Percent high school graduate or higher	55.3
Percent bachelor's degree or higher	7.3

Harrison County

Statue of Confederate General Thomas J. (Stonewall) Jackson in front of the Harrison County Courthouse in his native Clarksburg. (L. Victor Haines, WVU Photographic Services)

Harrison County is located in the north-central part of the state upon the Appalachian Plateau. The terrain of the county is rolling and hilly, except for some flat valleys located along the major streams. The county is drained by the West Fork River and its tributaries. The first known white settler in what is now Harrison County was John Simpson, who came to the mouth of Elk Creek on the West Fork River—the present-day site of Clarksburg—and erected a camp in 1764. By the early 1770's settlers became quite numerous in this vicinity, and in 1772 Nutter's Fort was built on Elk Creek for protection against the Indians.

Harrison County was formed in 1784 from part of Monongalia County. It took its name from Benjamin Harrison, the distinguished Virginian who was one of the signers of the Declaration of Independence and governor of Virginia from 1781 to 1784.

Harrison County is the "mother" of sixteen counties in northern West Virginia. In 1790 the population of Harrison County was 2,080.

The rich coal, gas, and petroleum reserves of the county began to be exploited after the turn of this century. The boom that this economic activity created caused the population to more than double from 1900 to 1920—rising from 27,690 in 1900, to 48,381 in 1910, and 74,793 in 1920. Glass factories also sprang up in the 1890's and early 1900's, utilizing the abundant natural gas of the county. Coal production was 126,594 tons in 1888, rose to 5,710,982 tons by 1920, and hit an all-time high of 12,744,276 tons in 1945. In 1983 production was 3,297,000 tons. The population of the county peaked in 1950 at 85,296. In 1990, population was just short of 70,000.

Clarksburg, the county seat, was established in 1785 and named for General George Rogers Clark, the Revolutionary War hero. Its population was 895 in 1860, rose to 9,201 in 1910, and jumped to 27,869 in 1920. In 1990 the city had a population of 18,059.

Lost Creek in 1992 was chosen one of five finalists from all over the US for the "Best Small Town in America Award."

Shinnston was first settled by Levi Shinn in 1773 and was first known as Shinn's Town. It was incorporated with its present name in 1877; population was 1,679 in 1920 and 3,059 in 1980.

Salem, located on Salem Fork, was formerly called New Salem. It was named for the town of Salem, New Jersey, where most of its original settlers had originated. Its population was 2,920 in 1920 and 2,063 in 1990. Salem College, now Salem-Teiku University, located at Salem, was chartered in 1888. It was founded by the Seventh Day Baptists.

Harrison County Notables

Herbert P. "Babe" Barna (1915-). Three-sport standout at WVU, went on to a 16-year pro baseball career.

Michael L. Benedum (1869-1959). Known as "the Great Wildcatter," he earned a fortune, much of which he returned to West Virginia through the Claude Worthington Benedum Foundation of Pittsburgh.

John S. Carlile (1817-1878). Leader of the statehood movement and the first United States Senator from West Virginia.

Nancy Grace Cornwell (1946-). Chosen West Virginia "Queen of the Century" at the State's Centennial in 1963.

Phyllis Curtin (1922-). Opera singer and teacher.

John W. Davis (1873-1955). Lawyer, congressman, diplomat, and Democratic candidate for President of the United States in 1924.

Nathan Goff (1843-1920). Soldier, jurist, and United States Senator from West Virginia 1913-1919.

Howard M. Gore (1877-1947). Governor of West Virginia 1925-1929.

Thomas (Stonewall) Jackson (1824-1863). Civil War general, considered one of the greatest military leaders of all time.

Jennings Randolph (1902-). US senator from West Virginia, 1958-1980. Chaired many important committees, was known as the "humanitarian senator."

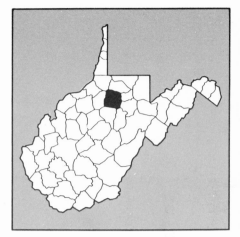

ECONOMIC PROFILE

Poverty status (all persons)	17.4%
65 and older	13.3%
Farms/value of farm products sold	554/$3.61 million
Retail sales	$478.29 million
Home ownership	74.0%
Value added by mining	$126.80 million
Median home value	$45,000
Median rent	$205/mo.

Joseph Johnson (1785-1877). Only ante-bellum governor of Virginia from a district west of the Alleghenies.

Melville Davisson Post (1871-1930). Author, best known for detective stories.

Joe Stydahar (1912-   ). WVU football star selected to Grantland Rice's all-time college and pro teams. First grid lineman to be drafted by pros.

Cyrus Vance (1917-   ). Lawyer and U.S. Secretary of State, 1977-1980.

Bibliography

Clarksburg-Harrison Bicentennial Commission. *Harrison County 76.* Clarksburg, 1976.

Davis, Dorothy. *History of Harrison County, West Virginia.* Clarksburg, American Association of University Women, 1970.

Haymond, Henry. *History of Harrison County, West Virginia; From The Early Days Of Northwestern Virginia To The Present.* Morgantown, Acme Publishing Co., 1910. Reprinted: Parsons, McClain Printing Co., 1973.

HARRISON COUNTY

Land in square miles	417
Total population	69,371
Percentage rural	39.4
Percentage female population	52.3
Percentage African-American population	1.4
Median age	36.9
Birth rate per 1,000 pop.	13.0
Percentage 65 and older	17.7
Median family income	$25,245

Educational attainment

Percent high school graduate or higher	70.6
Percent bachelor's degree or higher	13.5

Jackson County

Ferry crossing the Ohio River at Ravenswood. (L. Victor Haines, WVU Photographic Services)

Jackson County is located in the western part of West Virginia and borders on the Ohio River. The county's terrain is, for the most part, hilly and broken. However, there are large areas of flat bottomland along the Ohio River, Big Mill Creek, and the Big Sandy River. One early visitor to the area, and one of the first landowners in the region, was George Washington, who traveled through the area in 1770. The first permanent settlement was made in 1796 by three veterans of the Revolutionary War, James McDade, Benjamin Cox, and William Hannamon.

Jackson County was formed in 1831 from parts of Kanawha, Mason, and Wood counties. The county was named for Andrew Jackson, hero of the War of 1812 and seventh President of the United States. By 1840, the new county had a population of 4,890. Jackson County began to grow rapidly after the Civil War and the population reached 22,987 in 1900. Both oil and gas exploitation and the county's rich farmland contributed to this growth. The county's population then began to decline until the 1950's, when the population began to grow again. This renewal was given considerable impetus by Kaiser Aluminum and Chemical Corporation building a large aluminum plant near Ravenswood. By 1990, the county achieved a new population high of 25,938.

Jackson County hosts the annual Mountain State Arts and Craft Festival every Fourth of July week at Cedar Lakes FFA-FHA State Camp.

Ripley, established in 1832, is the county seat. It was named for Harry Ripley, a young minister, who had drowned nearby in the early 19th century. In 1990, the town had a population of 3,023.

Ravenswood is the county's largest town and economic center. The town was laid out in 1836 and officially established in 1852. The origin of the town's name is unclear. One explanation was that one of the founders was reading Sir Walter Scott's novel, *The Bride of Lammermore,* at the time and that he named the town for the book's hero, Lord Ravenswood. Today, the town has a population of 4,189.

Jackson County Notables

Andrew D. Hopkins (1857-1940). Eminent horticulturist, author of Hopkins' Bioclimatic Law.

Jesse Hughes (1750-1829). Scout, frontiersman, and famous Indian fighter.

Edythe L. Rowley (1900-1974). Social secretary for the White House under five presidents.

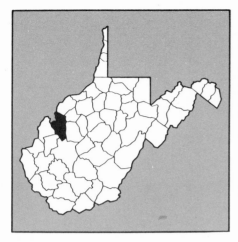

ECONOMIC PROFILE

Poverty status (all persons)	20.0%
65 and older	22.9%
Farms/value of farm products sold	679/$3.35 million
Retail sales	$100.04 million
Home ownership	78.4%
Value added by mining	NA
Median home value	$51,400
Median rent	$226/mo.

Bibliography

Delta Kappa Gamma Society International. Alpha Delta Chapter. Bicentennial Committee. *Early History of Pioneer Days in Jackson County: A History of Jackson County, Virginia (Becoming West Virginia June 20, 1863) Prior to 1900.* Marietta, Ohio, COMSERVCO, 1976.

Moore, Dean W. *Washington's Woods: A History of Ravenswood and Jackson County, West Virginia.* Parsons, McClain Printing Co., 1971.

O'Brien, Winnifred E. *Early Settlers and Their Contributions to Jackson County and Its County Seat, Ripley, West Virginia.* Ripley, Jackson County Public Library, 1979.

JACKSON COUNTY

Land in square miles	464
Total population	25,938
Percentage rural	72.2
Percentage female population	51.1
Percentage African-American population	0.1
Median age	35.7
Birth rate per 1,000 pop.	11.6
Percentage 65 and older	13.4
Median family income	$25,121

Educational attainment

Percent high school graduate or higher	65.4
Percent bachelor's degree or higher	8.7

Jefferson County

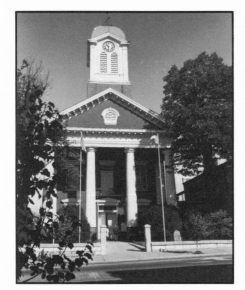

Above: Jefferson County Courthouse in Charles Town, built in 1836, was twice the scene of treason trials—abolitionist John Brown in 1859 and leaders of the coal miners' 1921 armed march in southern West Virginia. (L. Victor Haines, WVU Photographic Services)

Right: Shepherdstown, oldest community in West Virginia. (L. Victor Haines, WVU Photographic Services)

Jefferson County is the eastern-most of those counties comprising the Eastern Panhandle of West Virginia. It was created from Berkeley County in 1801 and named after Thomas Jefferson. The first white settlements were established in the area around present-day Shepherdstown about 1720. The excellent soil and favorable terrain made the area attractive and the population grew steadily. The county's population exceeded 11,000 by 1810 and reached 15,337 (including 4,341 slaves) in 1850. Conditions favored plantation agriculture, and large estates were developed. Many fine homes of estate owners still stand and bear witness to the wealth of the region.

Jefferson County suffered greatly during and immediately after the Civil War. The area was the scene of several battles and many skirmishes. The economy was disrupted by military action, while the abolition of slavery made plantation agriculture all but impossible. Readjustment and recovery were slow and painful. Population declined to 13,219 in 1870 and did not regain the 1850 level for several decades. Indeed, the county experienced relatively little growth until the late 1960's. At that time many individuals and concerns in the Washington area discovered the beauty and charm of nearby Jefferson County. The economy began to develop rapidly, while the population increased over 50 percent from 1970 to 1990, when it stood at 35,926.

Charles Town, the county seat, was chartered in 1786. It was named for Charles Washington, George Washington's brother, who laid out the town on his land. The population in 1990 was 3,122.

Harpers Ferry, located at the confluence of the Shenandoah and Potomac rivers, was settled in the 1730's. It was the scene of John Brown's raid in 1859, and is the site of Harpers Ferry National Historical Park, an increasingly important tourist attraction.

Shepherdstown is one of the oldest, perhaps the oldest, town in the state. First settlers arrived in the area about 1720, and the town was chartered as Mecklenberg in 1762. The name was changed in 1798 to Shepherd's Town, after an early settler, and to Shepherdstown in 1867. The town is the site of Shepherd College, a state-supported college founded in 1872. It has an enrollment of approximately 3,500 students. The population of Shepherdstown in 1990 was 1,287.

Jefferson County Notables

John Peale Bishop (1892-1944). Author and critic.

Martin R. Delany (1812-1885). Editor, physician, explorer, and the first black major in the U.S. Army.

Jefferson

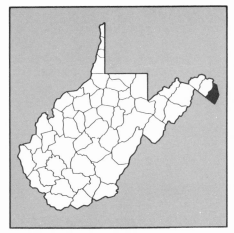

ECONOMIC PROFILE

Poverty status (all persons)	10.6%
65 and older	15.4%
Farms/value of farm products sold	363/$18.82 million
Retail sales	$118.43 million
Home ownership	71.9%
Value added by mining	NA
Median home value	$84,100
Median rent	$294/mo.

George W. Johnson (1869-1944). Member of US House of Representatives, 1923-25 and 1933-43.

Robert Lucas (1781-1853). Descendant of William Penn, served as general in War of 1812 and became governor of Ohio and Iowa.

Emmanuel W. Wilson (1844-1905). Governor of West Virginia, 1885-1890.

William L. Wilson (1843-1900). Established the first rural free delivery system as Postmaster General under President Cleveland.

Bibliography

Barry, Joseph. *The Strange Story of Harper's Ferry, With Legends of the Surrounding Country.* Martinsburg, Thompson Brothers, 1903. Reprinted: Shepherdstown, Shepherdstown Register, 1958.

Bushong, Millard K. *Historic Jefferson County.* Boyce, Va., Carr Publishing Co., 1972.

Dandridge, Danske Bedinger. *Historic Shepherdstown.* Charlottesville, Va., The Michie Co., 1910.

JEFFERSON COUNTY

Land in square miles	209
Total population	35,926
Percentage rural	83.3
Percentage female population	50.8
Percentage African-American population	7.4
Median age	32.7
Birth rate per 1,000 pop.	15.3
Percentage 65 and older	11.4
Median family income	$30,497

Educational attainment

Percent high school graduate or higher	68.2
Percent bachelor's degree or higher	16.9

Kanawha County

State Capitol. (Michael A. Powers, West Virginia Department of Commerce)

Kanawha County is located in the south-central part of the state. Its terrain is broken and hilly. The land is drained by the Kanawha, Elk, and Coal rivers and their tributaries.

Evidence for one of the oldest human occupations within the confines of the state was found at St. Albans in Kanawha County in 1968. At the site, located along the Kanawha River, projectile points of flint and other datable artifacts were found at a depth of 30 feet below the natural grade, proving that this area was occupied by a group of the so-called Paleo-Indians about 8,000 B.C. Indian burial mounds found in South Charleston, St. Albans, and Dunbar indicate that the area was occupied by the Adena or Hopewell peoples about the time of the birth of Christ.

The oldest known settlement in the county was made by Walter Kelly in 1773, who was killed by Indians that same year. There were few settlers in the area until the Battle of Point Pleasant in 1774 wrested control of the Kanawha River basin from Chief Cornstalk and the Shawnees. In 1787 George Clendenin, a veteran of the Battle of Point Pleasant, purchased lands at the mouth of the Elk River and in April of 1788, erected Fort Lee on a site now included within the confines of the city of Charleston.

Kanawha County was formed in 1788 from parts of Greenbrier and Montgomery (Virginia) counties and named for the Great Kanawha River. As originally formed, the county was about ten times its present size. Since its creation, 16 counties have been formed from it. In 1791, Daniel Boone (1734-1820) came to the Charleston area and was elected to the Virginia General Assembly to represent Kanawha County. In 1800, Kanawha County had a population of 3,239.

Kanawha County is underlaid with vast reserves of minerals—salt brine, coal, oil, and gas. The salt industry was the first important industry in the county. In 1808, Joseph Ruffner, who had occupied a large tract of land at the Salt Licks near Malden, succeeded in drilling a well to tap the rich reserves of salt brine below. From that year until about 1870, the salt industry was the major industry of the Kanawha County area. The technology and equipment developed for salt wells was easily adapted to drill deeper for gas and oil, and the county has long been an important producer of both. Large-scale commercial coal production began with the development of rail and river transportation systems in the 1870's. Coal production was 6,444,903 tons in 1910 and continued to climb, reaching 11,971,700 tons in 1970. In 1983, production was 7,179,299 tons.

Kanawha has been the most populous county in the state since 1880, when it surpassed Ohio County. From 32,466 in 1880, its population grew to 81,457 in 1910, and to 239,629 in 1950. It has dropped in recent years, however, and was 207,619 in 1990.

The chemical industry, centered in South Charleston, is one of the major employers in the county. Other important industries and sources of employment are glass and glassware, mine machinery, wholesale and retail sales, banking, and state government.

Charleston, the county seat, is located on the Kanawha River at the mouth of the Elk River. It was first settled in 1788 by Colonel George Clendenin, who named the town for his father, Charles. Charleston is the site of the West Virginia Capitol, seat of the state government, first located there by order of the State Legislature in 1870. However, in 1873, the Legislature approved the return of the capital to Wheeling, where it had been from 1863 to 1870. In 1885, after a plebiscite on the issue, the capital was finally relocated permanently in Charleston. The present Capitol

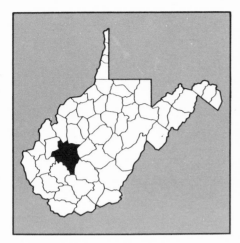

ECONOMIC PROFILE

Poverty status (all persons)	15.3%
65 and older	11.8%
Farms/value of farm products sold	7/$1.36 million
Retail sales	$1,504.69 million
Home ownership	68.5%
Value added by mining	$109.6 million
Median home value	$56,400
Median rent	$259/mo.

building was designed by famed architect Cass Gilbert and was dedicated in 1932.

Charleston had a population of 1,800 in 1860, 11,099 in 1900, 39,608 in 1920, and 57,287 in 1990. The University of Charleston, located on the south side of the Kanawha River across from the Capitol, was first established at Barboursville in 1888 by the Southern Methodists and relocated to Charleston in 1935. Until 1979, it was known as Morris Harvey College.

South Charleston was named for its position on the south side of the Kanawha River, opposite the city of Charleston. Within the town's borders lies one of the major chemical centers of the world. In 1920, it had a population of 3,650; by 1990, it had grown to a town of 13,645.

St. Albans, located along the Kanawha River at the mouth of the

KANAWHA COUNTY

Land in square miles	901
Total population	207,619
Percentage rural	29.1
Percentage female population	52.8
Percentage African-American population	6.6
Median age	36.7
Birth rate per 1,000 pop.	12.4
Percentage 65 and older	15.7
Median family income	$30,030

Educational attainment

Percent high school graduate or higher	72.4
Percent bachelor's degree or higher	17.6

Kanawha

Charleston, the state's largest urban area. (L. Victor Haines, WVU Photographic Services)

Coal River, was first known as Philippi, after an early settler, Phillip Thompson. Later, it was renamed Coalsmouth, then Kanawha City, and finally St. Albans in 1868 after a small town in Vermont. Its population was 2,825 in 1920; by 1990, it had a population of 11,194.

Dunbar was incorporated in 1921 and named for Dunbar Baines, a Charleston broker and lawyer. It had a population of 8,697 in 1990. West Virginia State College, located just west of Dunbar in the town of Institute, was chartered in 1891. It has an enrollment of almost 5,000.

Kanawha County Notables

Curtis H. Barnette (1935-   ). St. Albans native who became Chairman and CEO of Bethlehem Steel Corporation in 1992.

Becky Cain (1942-   ). St. Albans native, national president of the League of Women Voters in 1993.

William E. Chilton (1858-1939). United States Senator from West Virginia, 1911-1917.

William G. Conley (1866-1940). Governor of West Virginia, 1929-1933.

George H. Crumb (1929-   ). University of Pennsylvania composer who won the Pulitzer Prize for music.

Rod "Hot Rod" Hundley (1934-   ). All-state basketball player at Charleston High School, All-American at WVU.

John E. Kenna (1848-1893). United States Senator from West Virginia, 1883-1893.

William Alexander MacCorkle (1857-1930). Governor of West Virginia, 1893-1897.

Jack Maurice (1913-   ). Only West Virginia editor to win Pulitzer Prize for editorial writing (Charleston Daily Mail).

Arnold Miller (1923-1985). President of the United Mine Workers of America, 1972-1979.

Earl Morris (1909-1992). Noted attorney, was president of the American Bar Association.

Eugenia Price (1917-1996). Famed novelist (*Beloved Invader, New Moon Rising,* many others), born in Charleston.

Chapman J. Revercomb (1895-1979). Senator from West Virginia, 1943-1949 and 1956-1959.

Charles Ripper (1929-   ). Leading nature artist who has illustrated many books.

Monument to Booker T. Washington is on the State Capitol grounds in Charleston. The renowned black educator, founder of Tuskegee University, grew up at nearby Malden. (L. Victor Haines, WVU Photographic Services)

John Davison Rockefeller IV (1937-). Governor of West Virginia, 1977-1984. United States Senator 1985-

Mary Lee Settle (1918-). Novelist who won the National Book Award in 1978 for *Blood Tie.*

Booker T. Washington (1856-1915). Black educator and leader.

Jerry West (1938-). Star basketball player and coach. All-American at West Virginia University 1958, 1959, 1960. In 1991, the US Postal Service issued a commemorative envelope honoring West.

Harry K. "Cy" Young (1893-1972). Captained four different sports teams at Washington and Lee, elected to National Football Collegiate Hall of Fame.

Bibliography

DeGruyter, Julius A. *The Kanawha Spectator.* Charleston, 1953-1976. 2 volumes.

Goodall, Elizabeth J. "The Charleston Industrial Area: Development, 1797-1937." *West Virginia History, vol. 30* (October 1968).

Harris, Vernon B. *Great Kanawha: An Historical Outline.* Charleston, 1976.

Laidley, William S. *History of Charleston and Kanawha County, West Virginia, and Representative Citizens.* Chicago, Richmond-Arnold Publishing Co., 1911.

Lewis County

State 4-H Camp at Jackson's Mill, which was the first in the nation when it opened in 1921. (David R. Creel, WVU Photographic Services)

Lewis County is located in the central part of the state. The terrain of the county is hilly, with some rolling and flat land. Most of the county is drained by the West Fork River and its tributaries, though the northwestern section is drained by the tributaries of the Little Kanawha River.

The first white settlement in what is now Lewis County was made in 1770 by John Hacker, in the area now known as Hacker's Creek. The tide of migration into the area started after the Revolution and increased considerably after the Indian conflict was eliminated in the 1790's. The great increase in the number of settlers near the headwaters of the West Fork River led to the formation of Lewis County in 1816. It was created from a part of Harrison County and named for Colonel Charles Lewis, a famous soldier and leader among the Virginia pioneers, who was killed at the Battle of Point Pleasant in 1774. When first formed, Lewis County measured 1,754 square miles, but through subsequent losses in the formation of the neighboring counties of Braxton, Ritchie, Gilmer, and Upshur, it was reduced to slightly less than 400 square miles. In 1820, Lewis County had a population of 4,247.

In 1881, the Clarksburg, Weston and Glenville Transportation Company completed a narrow-gauge railroad line from Weston to Clarksburg. Soon thereafter, gas, oil, and glassmaking industries began their operations in the county. By 1900, Jane Lew in the northern part of the county was an important shipping point for gas and oil well supplies. Coal production began in 1907, when production was 6,191 tons. Production steadily increased thereafter, with 464,275 tons in 1950, 687,333 tons in 1970, and 811,000 tons in 1980. Over three-fourths of the 1980 total was mined at surface mines. The population of the county reached 20,455 in 1920 and peaked in 1940 at 22,271. In 1970 it had declined to 17,847, and in 1990 it was 17,223.

Weston, the county seat, is located on the West Fork River at the mouth of Stone Coal Creek. It was established in 1818 and was first named Preston in honor of Governor James P. Preston of Virginia. In 1819, the name was changed to Flesherville in honor of the first settler of the area. Later that same year, the name was finally changed to Weston. Weston Hospital, West Virginia's oldest and largest mental hospital, is located here. It was established in 1858 as the Trans-Allegheny Lunatic Asylum. The State 4H Camp, the first such in the country, is located at nearby Jackson's Mill.

Lewis County Notables

Roy Bird Cook (1886-1961). Historian and authority on Stonewall Jackson.

Andrew Edmiston (1892-1966). Member of US House of Representatives, 1933-43.

Gene H. "Red" Edwards (1904-1981). Was all-state in football and basketball at Weston High. Played in 1925 Rose Bowl. In 1926 was co-captain and quarterback at Notre Dame.

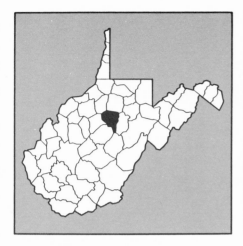

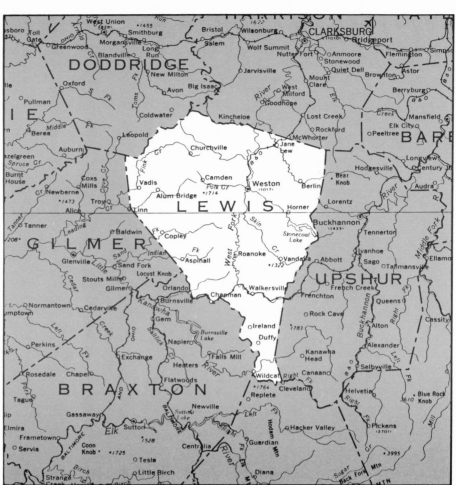

ECONOMIC PROFILE

Poverty status (all persons)	23.7%
65 and older	19.8%
Farms/value of farm products sold	335/$2.85 million
Retail sales	$68.56 million
Home ownership	69.8%
Value added by mining	NA
Median home value	$42,200
Median rent	$174/mo.

Rush D. Holt (1905-1955). United States Senator, 1935-1941.

Joseph A. J. Lightburn (1824-1901). Civil War General in the Union Army.

William Neely (1930-). Well-known author.

Bibliography

Cook, Roy Bird. *Lewis County in the Civil War, 1861-1865.* Charleston, Jarrett Printing Co., 1924.

Gilbert/Commonwealth. *Historic Resources Evaluation, Stonewall Jackson Lake Project, West Fork River, West Virginia.* (Prepared for) U.S. Department of the Army, Pittsburgh District, Corps of Engineers. Jackson, Mich., Gilbert/Commonwealth, 1980.

Smith, Edward Conrad. *A History of Lewis County, West Virginia.* Weston, The Author, 1920.

LEWIS COUNTY

Land in square miles	389
Total population	17,223
Percentage rural	71.0
Percentage female population	51.3
Percentage African-American population	0.3
Median age	36.5
Birth rate per 1,000 pop.	11.0
Percentage 65 and older	16.5
Median family income	$22,273

Educational attainment

Percent high school graduate or higher	62.1
Percent bachelor's degree or higher	8.2

Lincoln County

Charles Yeager, who was born in Lincoln County, became the first person to fly a plane faster than the speed of sound. He is the hero of Tom Wolfe's best-selling book, "The Right Stuff," which was made into a popular motion picture. (West Virginia and Regional History Collection, WVU Libraries)

Lincoln County is in the south west portion of West Virginia; the terrain is broken and hilly. The area began to be settled about 1800, when settlers carved out small farms. The region remained isolated and much of it sparsely settled for decades. The need to travel long distances over poor roads to reach a courthouse gave rise to increasing demands that a new county be formed. Thus Lincoln County was created in 1867 from parts of Boone, Cabell, Kanawha, and Putnam counties. The county was named after President Abraham Lincoln. Three years after its formation the new county had a population of 5,053.

Lincoln County's economy was from the first based on agriculture.

Tobacco has proved to be especially important as a cash crop. There was some coal mining in the early part of this century, with production reaching 327,000 tons in 1928. Mining declined sharply thereafter and is no longer significant. Oil and gas production have long provided some income and employment. The majority of the population depend for their livelihood upon agriculture or employment in the Huntington area. The population in 1990 was over 21,000.

Hamlin, the county seat, was probably named in honor of Hannibal Hamlin, Lincoln's vice president from 1860 to 1864. However, some authorities maintain that it was named for Leonidas L. Hamline, a prominent

Methodist clergyman. The site was first settled by David Stephenson in 1802 and chartered about 1867. Hamlin had a population of 1,030 in 1990.

Lincoln County Notables

Benjamin D. Alley (1898-1969). One of the nation's most popular vocalists in the era prior to World War II.

Charles Yeager (1923-   ). A Brigadier General in the U.S. Air Force and first jet pilot to break the sound barrier.

Bibliography

"Hardesty's Lincoln County." *West Virginia Heritage Encyclopedia.* Supplemental Series, vol. 7.

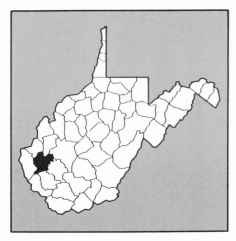

ECONOMIC PROFILE

Poverty status (all persons)	33.8%
65 and older	24.9%
Farms/value of farm products sold	304/$1.14 million
Retail sales	$33.69 million
Home ownership	77.1%
Value added by mining	NA
Median home value	$38,200
Median rent	$172/mo.

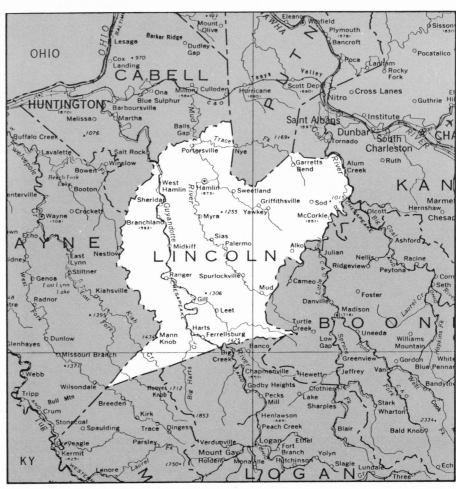

LINCOLN COUNTY

Land in square miles	439
Total population	21,382
Percentage rural	100
Percentage female population	50.9
Percentage African-American population	0.0
Median age	33.4
Birth rate per 1,000 pop.	14.4
Percentage 65 and older	12.5
Median family income	$16,868

Educational attainment

Percent high school graduate or higher	49.1
Percent bachelor's degree or higher	4.7

Logan County

Hatfield Cemetery with statue of Devil Anse, who was made famous by the Hatfield-McCoy family feud. (L. Victor Haines, WVU Photographic Services)

Logan County lies in the south western part of West Virginia. Most of the county's rough, hilly terrain is drained by the Guyandotte River. The first permanent European settlement was made by James Workman in 1794. Another important early homestead was made by William Dingess in 1799. In the years that followed, a steady trickle of pioneers moved into the region to establish farms. In 1824, Logan County was created from parts of Cabell, Giles, Kanawha, and Tazewell counties. The county was named for Logan, chief of the Mingo tribe. By 1830, the county had a population of 3,680.

Logan County grew very slowly. The area was remote and transportation was difficult in good weather and almost impossible in bad. Logging and farming provided the only significant sources of income. The existence of vast coal deposits in Logan County had been recognized since at least the 1850's. However, the coal was of no commercial value without adequate transportation, and that the area lacked. Thus, as late as 1900 the county had a population of only 6,955.

By 1900 the demand for coal had convinced investors that the opening of the Logan coal fields would prove profitable. The Chesapeake and Ohio Railroad reached what was then the village of Logan Court House in September, 1904, and soon developed an extensive network throughout the area. Coal production began to expand at an enormous rate. In 1910, over 2.2 million tons were produced; ten years later, production was 9.8 million tons Coal production peaked in 1950 with 19,545,186 tons and then began to decline. Production in 1983 was approximately nine million tons. Logan County's population has reflected the fortune of the coal industry. Population increased approximately sixfold from 1900 to 1920, when it reached 41,006. It peaked at over 77,000 in 1950 and then declined to 46,269 in 1970, and 43,032 in 1990.

This county was the scene of a tragedy gaining national attention February 25, 1972, when an earthen dam collapsed on Buffalo Creek, resulting in a wall of water that killed 118 people with seven more listed as missing.

Logan, the county seat, had a population in 1990 of 2,026. Earlier names for the town were Lawnville and Aracoma. The town was no more than a small village until the arrival of the railroad in 1904.

Logan County Notables

Joanne Dru (Joanne LaCoque) (1923-1996). A leading motion picture actress for three decades.

Thomas Dunn English (1819-1902). Author of the ballad "Ben Bolt." He lived in Lawnville (now Logan) during the period 1852-1856 and was the first mayor of the town.

Charlie O. Erickson, Jr. (1914-1993). Multimillionaire TV cable industry pioneer who has given millions to the construction of alumni centers at eleven West Virginia institutions of higher learning.

Peter Marshall (LaCoque, Dru's brother) (1925-   ). Prominent TV master of ceremonies.

Mark C. Workman (1930-1983). Basketball star at Charleston High School and at WVU.

Bibliography

Spence, Robert Y. *The Land of the Guyandot: A History of Logan County.* Detroit, Mich., Harlo Press, 1976.

Swain, George T. *History of Logan County, West Virginia.* Logan, G. T. Swain, 1927.

Thurmond, Walter R. *The Logan Coal Field of West Virginia. A Brief History.* Morgantown, West Virginia University Library, 1964.

Logan

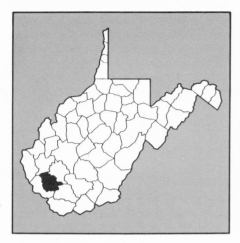

ECONOMIC PROFILE

Poverty status (all persons)	27.7%
65 and older	19.3%
Farms/value of farm products sold	27/$461,000
Retail sales	$215.52 million
Home ownership	73.2%
Value added by mining	$277.4 million
Median home value	$42,100
Median rent	$196/mo.

LOGAN COUNTY

Land in square miles	456
Total population	43,032
Percentage rural	92.3
Percentage female population	51.8
Percentage African-American population	3.2
Median age	33.9
Birth rate per 1,000 pop.	11.5
Percentage 65 and older	12.6
Median family income	$21,100

Educational attainment

Percent high school graduate or higher	53.4
Percent bachelor's degree or higher	6.3

Marion County

Pricketts Fort, reconstructed eighteenth-century settlement. The original fort was built in 1774 to protect nearby settlers from Indian attack. (L. Victor Haines, WVU Photographic Services)

Marion County is located in the north-central part of the state. The terrain of the county is hilly, except for some flat land along river valleys. The principal streams of the county are the Monongahela River, which flows northward through the county, and the West Fork and Tygart Valley rivers. The first known white settlers came to Marion County just after the French and Indian War (1758-63). During the Indian raids of 1774, settlers in this area abandoned their homes and gathered at the settlement of Jacob Prickett, where they erected a large stockade and fort. Today Pricketts Fort is a state park.

Marion County was created in 1842 from parts of Monongalia and Harrison counties and named in honor of General Francis Marion of Revolutionary War fame. In 1850, the population of the county was 10,552. Large-scale coal operations began in the 1880's, when mines were opened at Fairmont and Monongah. By 1888, coal production exceeded 250,000 tons, and reached the million-ton level in 1894. In 1916, production was 6,189,891 tons and has remained in the six to nine million-ton range for most of the years thereafter. In 1983, coal production was 7,957,938 tons.

The development of coal, oil, and gas industries brought great wealth to Marion County. Population increased in response to the new opportunities for employment and more than doubled between 1900 (32,430) and 1930 (66,655). The county's population peaked at 71,521 in 1950. "King Coal" also has brought great grief to Marion County. Monongah was the scene of the worst coal mine disaster in US history December 6, 1907, when 361 miners lost their lives in an underground explosion. Another explosion, in a Farmington mine, resulted in 78 deaths.

Fairmont, the county seat, was established in 1820 and first named Middletown. It was chartered in 1843 as Fairmont, the name being a contraction of Fair Mountain. In 1900, it had a population of 5,655; by 1920, it had grown to a town of 17,851 inhabitants. In 1990, the town had a population of 20,210. Fairmont State College was founded in 1865 as a private school, but it became a state institution in 1867 as Fairmont State Normal School. The college has an enrollment of approximately 6,600.

Mannington, located on Pyles' Fork, was formerly known as Koontown. It was renamed and chartered in 1856. In 1920, it had a population of 3,673 in 1990, the population was 2,184.

Marion County Notables

Aretus Brooks Fleming (1830-1923). Governor of West Virginia, 1890-1893.

Frank "Gunner" Gatski (1923-). Football star for Marshall and all-pro with the Cleveland Browns.

Camden Eli "Cam" Henderson (1890-1956). Great basketball and football coach at Marshall, Muskingum, and Davis and Elkins.

Robert L. "Sam" Huff (1934-). All-American football player at WVU and all-pro in NFL and businessman.

John Knowles (1926-). Novelist.

Russell D. "Russ" Meredith (1897-1970). Star grid tackle at Fairmont High School and All-American at WVU.

Ephraim F. Morgan (1869-1950). Governor of West Virginia, 1921-1925.

Matthew M. Neely (1874-1958). United States Senator and Governor of West Virginia, 1941-1945.

Francis H. Pierpont (1814-1899). Leader of the statehood movement and governor of the restored government of Virginia.

Mary Lou Retton (1968-). Olympic gold medalist in gymnastics.

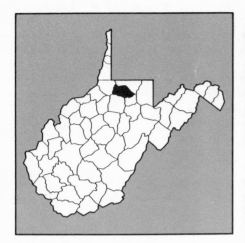

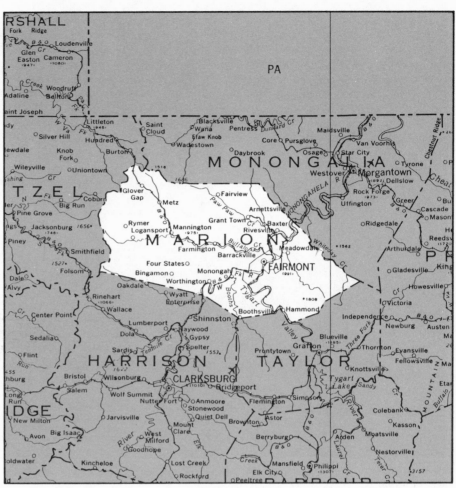

ECONOMIC PROFILE

Poverty status	
(all persons)	19.0%
65 and older	12.7%
Farms/value of farm products sold	362/$1.85 million
Retail sales	$317.50 million
Home ownership	75.5%
Value added by mining	NA
Median home value	$42,300
Median rent	$201/mo.

Clarence W. Watson (1864-1940). Coal operator and United States Senator 1911-1913.

Fielding H. "Hurry-Up" Yost (1871-1946). One of the great college football coaches of all time (176-33-10), primarily at Michigan and Stanford.

Bibliography

Balderson, Walter L. *Fort Prickett Frontier and Marion County.* Fairmont, 1977.

Dunnington, George A. and Lott, Richard P. *History of Marion County (1842-1880)* reprinted 1992 by Marion County Historical Society, Fairmont, W.Va.

Fairmont High School, Class of 1916. *Marion County In The Making.* Fairmont, J. O. Watson, 1917.

Lough, Glenn D. *Now And Long Ago: A History Of The Marion County Area.* Morgantown- Morgantown Printing and Binding Co., 1969.

MARION COUNTY

Land in square miles	456
Total population	57,249
Percentage rural	64.7
Percentage female population	53.4
Percentage African-American population	3.2
Median age	37.3
Birth rate per 1,000 pop.	11.5
Percentage 65 and older	18.3
Median family income	$25,963

Educational attainment

Percent high school graduate or higher	71.4
Percent bachelor's degree or higher	12.5

Marshall County

Grave Creek Mound at Moundsville, largest Indian burial mound east of the Mississippi River. (L. Victor Haines, WVU Photographic Services)

Marshall County is part of West Virginia's Northern Panhandle. Except for the flat Ohio River Valley, the terrain is generally rolling and hilly. The first white man known to have explored the area was Christopher Gist in 1751. The first settlement made within the county was by John Wetzel in 1769. The settlers who followed Wetzel relied upon Fort Henry, at what is today Wheeling, for protection from Indian raids. Marshall County was formed from Ohio County in 1835. The county was named for John Marshall, Chief Justice of the U. S. Supreme Court. By 1840, the county had a population of 6,937.

Marshall County's economy remained largely agricultural until well after the Civil War. However, by 1890, manufacturing and the production of coal and gas had become increasingly important. The expanding economic base caused population to grow from 20,735 in 1890 to over 32,000 by 1910. Manufacturing and coal mining are now the mainstays of the economy. Production of coal has increased rapidly in recent years, from less than a million tons per year in the 1950's to over five million tons today.

Moundsville, the county seat and the county's largest town, with a population of 10,753 in 1990 is at the mouth of Grave Creek along the Ohio River. The first settlement here was made in 1770 by Joseph Tomlinson who established a town on his land which he called Elizabethtown, after his wife. It and an adjacent town were consolidated as Moundsville in 1866. The town received its name from the gigantic mound built by the Adena people thousands of years ago. The Delf Norona Museum near the site contains artifacts from and exhibits about the mound and its builders. Moundsville is also the site of the West Virginia Penitentiary, which was established in 1866 and closed in 1995. And at New Vrindaban is the Palace of Gold, built in recent years by the Hare Krishna religious community.

Marshall County Notables

William A. Dalzell (1890-1971). A founder of the Fostoria Glass Company, long a Marshall county industrial mainstay.

Arch A. Moore, Jr. (1923-). Governor of West Virginia, 1969-1977, 1985-89.

Delf Norona (1895-1974). Historian and collector.

Gerald and Barbara Plants. Organizers of the McCreary Cemetery Preservation Foundation of Moundsville to preserve the burying places of the famous Wetzel pioneers.

Marshall

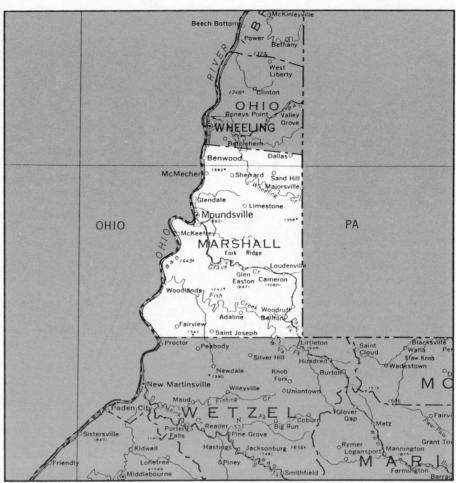

ECONOMIC PROFILE

Poverty status (all persons)	16.0%
65 and older	13.7%
Farms/value of farm products sold	425/$3.38 million
Retail sales	$166.45 million
Home ownership	77.9%
Value added by mining	NA
Median home value	$42,700
Median rent	$182/mo.

Sam Shaw (1874-1957) and *Sam Shaw, Jr. (1914-1995)*. The elder helped his father found *The Moundsville Echo* in 1891; the younger published *The Echo* until his death in 1995.

Lewis Wetzel (1763-1808). Frontiersman and Indian fighter.

Bibliography

Allman, Clarence B. *Lewis Wetzel, Indian Fighter*. New York: Devin Adair, 1961 (being reprinted by the Plants, see above.)

Boyd, Peter. *History of Northern West Virginia Panhandle, Embracing Ohio, Marshall, Brooke, and Hancock Counties*. Topeka, Kansas, Historical Publishing Co.,1927.2 vol.

Powell, Scott. *History of Marshall County from Forest to Field*. Moundsville, 1925.

MARSHALL COUNTY

Land in square miles	305
Total population	37,356
Percentage rural	50.1
Percentage female population	51.5
Percentage African-American population	0.5
Median age	36.6
Birth rate per 1,000 pop.	11.8
Percentage 65 and older	15.2
Median family income	$26,974

Educational attainment

Percent high school graduate or higher	70.9
Percent bachelor's degree or higher	9.7

Mason County

Point Pleasant is where the Kanawha River flows into the Ohio River. A state park is located at the confluence. (Gerald S. Ratliff, West Virginia Department of Commerce)

Mason County is one of the Ohio Valley counties on West Virginia's western border. The Ohio and Kanawha river bottoms are wide and the hills relatively low. In 1770, a group of surveyors, among them George Washington, surveyed the north bank of the Kanawha in what is now Mason County. The decisive battle of Lord Dunmore's War was fought at Point Pleasant on October 10, 1774. The battle of Point Pleasant was the climax of the conflict between the confederated Indians under the Shawnee chieftain Cornstalk and the colonial forces under General Andrew Lewis. The result was a victory for the Virginia colonists and the opening of the area for permanent settlers. It has been called the first battle of the Revolution.

Mason County was formed in 1804 from the western part of Kanawha County. The county was named in honor of George Mason (1725-1792), Virginia land owner and statesman. In 1810, the county had a population of 1,991. The area was attractive to settlers because the river bottoms were fertile and easily cultivated. The Ohio and Kanawha provided inexpensive transportation for such local products as lumber and salt. A significant boat-building industry had developed by 1860, at which date the population of the county was slightly over 9,000.

Mason County experienced substantial growth during the two decades after the Civil War. The population reached 22,296 in 1880 and has remained close to that level ever since. A modest coal industry began to develop at the turn of the century, with annual production climbing to the 500,000-ton level in 1960. However, coal production declined rapidly thereafter and is no longer significant. Its place in the economy has been taken by the growth of light industries.

Point Pleasant, the county seat, is located at the confluence of the Ohio and Kanawha rivers. The origin of the town's name is unclear. Some sources state that the site was named for General Lewis's camp during Lord Dunmore's War; others maintain that the name was given it by George Washington in 1770. Permanent settlers came to the spot in the 1780's, but it was not until 1833 that the community was incorporated as a town. In 1990, Point Pleasant had a population of 4,996.

Mason County Notables
Gus R. Douglass (1927-   ). Longtime WV Commissioner of Agriculture, former president of Future Farmers of America (FFA).

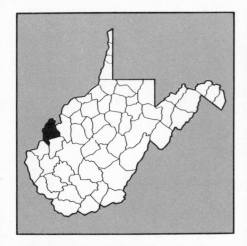

ECONOMIC PROFILE

Poverty status (all persons)	22.1%
65 and older	18.1%
Farms/value of farm products sold	709/$13.46 million
Retail sales	$71.12 million
Home ownership	78.5%
Value added by mining	NA
Median home value	$44,800
Median rent	$177/mo.

Charles E. (1852-1935) and Robert L. Hogg (1893-). Father and son, both born in Pt. Pleasant and both served in US House of Representatives.

Virgil A. Lewis (1848-1912). Historian and educator.

John McCausland (1836-1927). Confederate Brigadier General who burned Chambersburg, Pa. in 1864.

Michael J. Owens (1859-1923). Inventor and major figure in the glass industry.

Bibliography

"Hardesty's Mason County." *West Virginia Heritage Encyclopedia.* Supplemental Series, vol. 5.

History of the Great Kanawha Valley With Family History and Biographical Sketches. Madison, Wis., Brant, Fuller, & Co., 1891. 2 vol.

Lewis, Virgil A. *History of the Battle of Point Pleasant.* Charleston, The Tribune Printing Co., 1909.

MASON COUNTY

Land in square miles	433
Total population	25,178
Percentage rural	80.2
Percentage female population	51.4
Percentage African-American population	0.4
Median age	35.8
Birth rate per 1,000 pop.	11.6
Percentage 65 and older	14.1
Median family income	$24,125

Educational attainment

Percent high school graduate or higher	61.1
Percent bachelor's degree or higher	6.8

McDowell County

McDowell County Courthouse in Welch, which was built in 1895. (C. E. Turley)

McDowell County is the most southern of West Virginia's counties. The majority of the county lies in the drainage basin of the Tug Fork branch of the Big Sandy River. The terrain is rugged. Permanent settlers began to enter the area starting in the 1790's, but they remained few in number for many decades.

In 1858, McDowell County was created from Tazewell (Virginia) County. The county was named after James McDowell, Governor of Virginia from 1843 through 1845. The county had a population of 1,535 in 1860, but the region was too rugged and remote to be attractive to settlers. The population grew very slowly, reaching only 3,074 by 1880. Many people were aware of the county's rich coal fields, but the development of a coal industry had to await the arrival of the railroad.

The Norfolk and Western Railway started to push its lines west through McDowell County about 1885. Mines began to be opened on the main line and then on branch lines. One of the nation's greatest coal booms had begun. Coal production was 2.4 million tons in 1895 and grew to 12.1 million tons in 1910. Production increased almost every year thereafter and peaked at 26,494,300 tons in 1947. It then began to decline fairly steadily and was 6.1 million tons in 1983. The rapid development of the coal industry created many jobs and thousands of people moved into the area. McDowell County's population increased from 7,300 in 1890 to 47,856 in 1910, and was over 90,000 by 1930. Population peaked in 1950 at 98,887 and has since declined, reflecting the decline in coal production.

Jolo made the national news in 1992 with a three-day revival at the Church of the Lord Jesus, complete with rattlesnake handling under Pastor Dewey Chafin.

Welch, the county seat since 1892, is located at the confluence of Elkhorn Creek and Tug River. The town is named for Capt. Isaiah Welch, who surveyed the area. The village of Peeryville (now English) had been designated as the seat when the county was formed. The city in 1990 had a population of 3,028.

McDowell County Notables

Edward J. Berwind (1848-1936). A leading coal entrepreneur for whom the city of Berwind is named.

Leo Wesley Byrd (1937-   ). Born in Kimball, overcame polio at 12 to star in basketball for Huntington High School (all-state captain) and Marshall University where he was All-American.

Jack L. Hancock (1930-   ). Born in Welch, WVU graduate, retired US Army major general has had a successful banking career.

Henry D. Hatfield (1875-1962). Governor of West Virginia, 1913-1917, United States Senator, 1929-1935.

Ernest Hogan (1915-   ). Davy native, philanthropist who was President and CEO of the Peoples Security Life Insurance Company.

Bibliography

Daughters of the American Revolution. West Virginia. Col. Andrew Donnally Chapter. *McDowell County History; A Pictorial History of McDowell County, West Virginia, Covering Both the Old and the New.* Fort Texas, University Supply & Equipment Co., 1959.

McDowell County Centennial, Inc. *McDowell County Centennial, 1858-1958.* Welch 1958.

Tams, W. P., Jr. *The Smokeless Coal Fields of West Virginia: A Brief History.* Morgantown, West Virginia University Press, 1963.

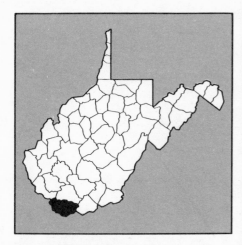

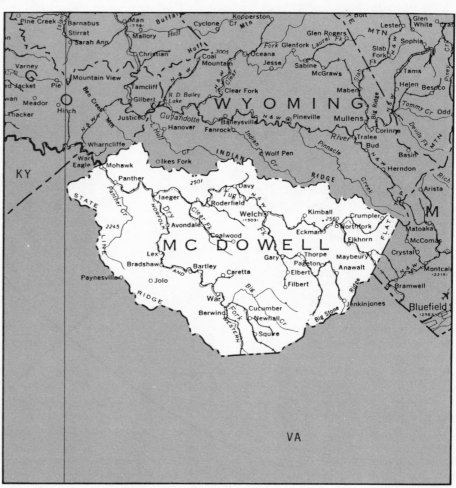

ECONOMIC PROFILE

Poverty status	
(all persons)	37.7%
65 and older	20.7%
Farms/value of farm products sold	12/No data
Retail sales	$120.98 million
Home ownership	78.7%
Value added by mining	$66.8 million
Median home value	$15,800
Median rent	$139/mo.

MCDOWELL COUNTY

Land in square miles	535
Total population	35,233
Percentage rural	91.3
Percentage female population	52.9
Percentage African-American population	13.5
Median age	34.0
Birth rate per 1,000 pop.	14.6
Percentage 65 and older	14.8
Median family income	$15,756

Educational attainment

Percent high school graduate or higher	42.3
Percent bachelor's degree or higher	4.6

Mercer County

Above: Edward Cooper House in Bramwell Historic District. After a coal field opened nearby in the late nineteenth century, many of the operators built ornate houses in Bramwell, which at one time claimed to have more millionaires per capita than any other American community. (Beth Hager)

Right: Mercer County Courthouse in Princeton, built in 1931, was the fifth on this site. The north and south facades contain carved stone friezes depicting occupations and industries in the county. (C. E. Turley)

Mercer County is one of the southernmost of West Virginia's 55 counties. The county is mountainous and nearly all of it lies above 2,000 feet. The principal rivers are the Bluestone and East rivers. White settlement began about 1775, but proceeded quite slowly, as the area was too remote and rugged to be very attractive to settlers. Mercer County was formed in 1837 from parts of Giles and Tazewell counties of Virginia and was named after General Hugh Mercer (1725-1777), a Revolutionary War hero. Three years after its formation Mercer County had a population of 2,233.

Mercer County remained a rural area for many years. In 1880, its population was only 7,467. The existence of great coal fields in the county was well known, but their development required rail transportation. Starting in 1881, the Norfolk and Western Railway began to push into the area. Mine after mine was opened and thousands of people moved in to take advantage of the new employment opportunities.

Coal production exceeded one million tons per year by 1900 and was well over two million tons by 1910. During the 1920's, Mercer County's coal production averaged over three million tons per year. It then began to decline and is now well under the million tons per year level. Population reflected coal production, increasing more than five-fold between 1880 and 1910. Population reached almost 50,000 in 1920 and peaked at 75,013 in 1950.

There are two state-supported colleges in Mercer County. The first was Concord College, established in 1872. The school is located in the town of Athens and enrolls some 3,000 students. The second was Bluefield State College, founded in 1895 to serve the black population of the region. It was integrated after 1954 and also has an enrollment of approximately 3,000.

Bluefield is the county's largest city, with a population of 12,700. The city was named for the bluegrass or flowers in the area. It came into being as a result of the opening of the Pocahontas coal fields in 1883. The town did not exist in 1880; by 1890, it had a population of 1,776, which grew to over 11,000 by 1910. Bluefield became the transportation, banking, and commercial center for the area and has remained such.

Princeton, the county seat, was established in 1837 and named after the Revolutionary War battle in which General Hugh Mercer was killed. The town remained a mere village for decades and was all but destroyed during the Civil War. In 1890, it had a population of 320. The development of the area's coal industry caused Princeton to grow rapidly. Its population was 3,027 in 1910 and more than double that ten years later. The present population is approximately 7,000.

Mercer County Notables

Roy *"Legs"* Hawley (1901-1954). Sports luminary who was All-American basketball player at Bluefield High School, then star and captain at WVU where he was athletic director, 1938-1954.

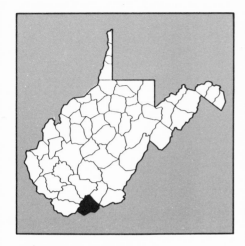

ECONOMIC PROFILE

Poverty status (all persons)	20.4%
65 and older	15.3%
Farms/value of farm products sold	358/$1.86 million
Retail sales	$404.31 million
Home ownership	76.3%
Value added by mining	$13.6 million
Median home value	$44,600
Median rent	$212/mo.

James Key (1917-). As did his father and mother (see Gilmer County) he served in the US House of Representatives, 1965-73.

John Shively Knight (1894-1981). After a long editorial career, founder and chairman of the Knight Newspaper Chain.

Hugh Ike Shott (1866-1953). Newspaper publisher, Congressman, 1929-1933, and United States Senator, 1942-1943.

Bibliography

Becker, Martha Jane. *The Diary of a Millionaire Coal Town - Bramwell.* Available from Books, PO Box 42, Bracey, VA 23919.

Johnston, David E. *A History of Middle New River Settlements and Contiguous Territory.* Huntington, Standard Printing & Publishing Co., 1906.

McCormick, Kyle. *The Story of Mercer County.* Charleston, Charleston Printing Co., 1957.

Rankin, John Rogers. *The Early History and Development of Bluefield, West Virginia.* Radford, Va., Commonwealth Press, 1976.

MERCER COUNTY

Land in square miles	420
Total population	64,980
Percentage rural	69.5
Percentage female population	53.1
Percentage African-American population	6.4
Median age	36.4
Birth rate per 1,000 pop.	12.5
Percentage 65 and older	16.6
Median family income	$24,020

Educational attainment

Percent high school graduate or higher	63.1
Percent bachelor's degree or higher	11.6

Mineral County

Potomac State College of West Virginia University, the state's only two-year residential college at Keyser. (David R. Creel, WVU Photographic Services)

Mineral County lies in the Eastern Panhandle of the state. It is divided into two topographical sections separated by the great backbone of the Allegheny Front—the western section, drained by many small tributaries of the North Branch of the Potomac, is part of the Appalachian Plateau and contains the coal-bearing regions; the eastern section, drained by Patterson and New creeks, which also flow into the North Branch, is part of the Ridge and Valley Province, and contains the richest farmland in the county.

The area which became Mineral County once belonged to Lord Fairfax, an English nobleman who inherited approximately 2,800 square miles of property in the Potomac River basin. In 1754, Hampshire County was created, and until 1866 Mineral County would remain part of Hampshire and share its history. The plantation sys-

tem of agriculture, so common in many Virginia counties, never took hold in the area now known as Mineral County; instead, small, independently owned holdings prevailed. The abundance of wood, coal, and iron ore in the western part of the county attracted small industries.

After the Civil War, the West Virginia Legislature divided rebellious Hampshire County and in 1866 created Mineral County, naming it for the rich mineral deposits of coal and iron ore found there. In 1870, the population of the county was 6,332. Population grew slowly but steadily and reached 26,097 in 1990.

Coal production began soon after the Civil War. Spurred by a network of railroads that connected the coal fields in the eastern part of the county to the Baltimore and Ohio main line, production increased to 524,852 tons in 1888 and rose to a peak of 961,714

tons in 1910. However, production declined to 164,402 in 1940 and was negligible by 1960. The development of surface mining during the 1970's caused a sharp increase in production to over 350,000 tons by 1980. The largest single employer in the county is the West Virginia Pulp and Paper Company.

Keyser, the county seat, was first known as Paddytown in honor of Patrick McCarthy, who settled here in 1760. It was renamed Keyser in 1874, for a vice president of the B & O. Its population was 2,536 in 1900; 6,003 in 1920; and 5,870 in 1990. Potomac State College, located at Keyser, was chartered in 1901 as a preparatory school for West Virginia University. In 1921, it became a two-year college. This branch of West Virginia University has an enrollment of approximately 1,200.

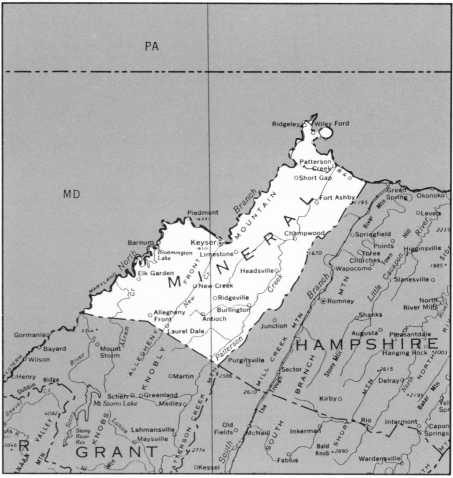

ECONOMIC PROFILE

Poverty status	
(all persons)	14.8%
65 and older	16.4%
Farms/value of farm products sold	315/$3.54 million
Retail sales	$68.26 million
Home ownership	77.5%
Value added by mining	$10.9 million
Median home value	$49,300
Median rent	$196/mo.

Mineral County Notables

Henry Gassaway Davis (1823-1916). US Senator (1871-1883) who ran for vice president in 1904.

Bess Johnson (1915-). An early radio star ("Lady Esther"), said to have appeared on more than 10,000 shows.

Harley O. Staggers (1907-1991). United States Congressman, 1949-1981.

Bibliography

Mineral County Heritage Society. *Mineral County, West Virginia: Family Traits, Tracks, and Trails, 1980.* Published by Robert L. Rummer, Sr., for the Society, 1980.

Wolfe, William W. *History of Keyser, West Virginia, 1737-1913.* Keyser, Keyprint, 1974.

MINERAL COUNTY

Land in square miles	329
Total population	26,697
Percentage rural	66.8
Percentage female population	51.6
Percentage African-American population	2.8
Median age	35.3
Birth rate per 1,000 pop.	12.6
Percentage 65 and older	14.7
Median family income	$26,895

Educational attainment

Percent high school graduate or higher	72.8
Percent bachelor's degree or higher	10.4

Mingo County

Above: West Virginia's hilly terrain makes highway building very expensive as this construction project in Mingo County indicates. (Mark Francis, Williamson Daily News)

Right: Tug Valley Chamber of Commerce in Williamson is appropriately housed in an office made of coal. (Mark Francis, Williamson Daily News)

Mingo County is located on the southwest border of West Virginia. It is a mountainous county and rich with coal deposits. The names of the first settlers are unknown to history, but they probably entered the area in the early 1790's. The region was sparsely settled for decades, its mountainous terrain and lack of transportation making it unattractive to settlers. The few inhabitants eked out a living by farming, lumbering, and hunting.

The existence of vast coal deposits had been recognized as early as the 1850's. However, coal is of little value without transportation, and the rugged terrain made the building of railroads difficult and costly. Thus, the area was undeveloped so long as ample supplies of coal were available elsewhere. By 1890, the increasing demand for coal made the southwestern West Virginia coal fields attractive to investors. In 1889, the Norfolk and Western began construction of what was known as the Ohio Extension, which reached Kenova on the Ohio

River in 1893. It had become obvious that the area was on the verge of an economic boom, and local citizens wished to gain more control of their affairs. In 1895, they succeeded in having Mingo County formed from Logan County. Some 11,359 people lived in the new county by 1900.

Coal mining on a large scale began with the arrival of the railroads. Production increased from 95,279 tons in 1895 to over 400,000 tons five years later, and hit two million tons in 1910. Coal production reached the five million-ton level in 1930 and, with some variations, has remained there. The rapidly expanding economy provided increased employment opportunities, both in and out of the mines. The population doubled from 1910 to 1930, when it was 38,319. Population peaked in 1950 at over 47,000, and has since declined as mechanization has reduced labor requirements in the coal industry.

Mingo County has seen more than its share of violence. What is now Mingo County was the scene of the

Hatfield-McCoy feud, doubtless the most notorious of the Appalachian feuds. In the 1920's it was also the scene of bitter and bloody disputes between miners and operators. Names such as Baldwin-Felts, Syd Hatfield, and the Matewan Massacre have become part of the folklore of the region.

Williamson is the county seat. In 1890, the site was only a cornfield, but by 1892, Williamson was incorporated as a town by Wallace J. Williamson, who owned the land. The town became a commercial and transportation center for the coal industry. Population grew rapidly and peaked at 9,410 in 1930. The 1990 population was 4,154.

Mingo County Notables
James "Buck" H. Harless (1919-). Businessman and philanthropist.

Anderson (Devil Anse) Hatfield (1839-1921). Patriarch of the Hatfield clan.

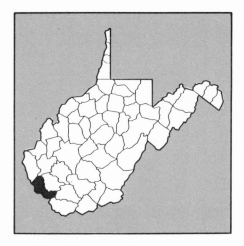

ECONOMIC PROFILE

Poverty status (all persons)	30.9%
65 and older	18.4%
Farms/value of farm products sold	4/No data
Retail sales	$128.62 million
Home ownership	72.8%
Value added by mining	$291.6 million
Median home value	$39,400
Median rent	$193/mo.

John Hendrickson (1952-). TV entrepreneur who originated the Discovery Channel and the Learning Channel.

Bibliography

Conner, Robert and Ruel Foster. *Buck Harless, A Biography.* Morgantown, W.Va: West Virginia University Press, 1992.

Rice, Otis K. *The Hatfields and McCoys.* Lexington, Ky., The University Press of Kentucky, 1978.

Smith, Nancy Sue. *An Early History of Mingo County,* West Virginia. Williamson, Williamson Printing Co., 1960.

Williamson Chamber of Commerce. *Williamson, West Virginia, "Heart of the Billion Dollar Coal Field."* Williamson, 1931.

MINGO COUNTY

Land in square miles	424
Total population	33,739
Percentage rural	87.7
Percentage female population	51.2
Percentage African-American population	2.4
Median age	31.1
Birth rate per 1,000 pop.	14.9
Percentage 65 and older	10.4
Median family income	$19,643

Educational attainment

Percent high school graduate or higher	50.4
Percent bachelor's degree or higher	6.6

Monongalia County

Woodburn Circle at West Virginia University, where university education began in West Virginia in 1867, has been entered in the National Register of Historic Places. The three buildings are (from left) Martin Hall (1870), Woodburn Hall (1876), and Chitwood Hall (1893). (L. Victor Haines, WVU Photographic Services)

Monongalia County is located in the north-central part of the state. It lies on the Appalachian Plateau and has a terrain that is more hilly than mountainous. The land is drained by the Monongahela and Cheat rivers and their tributaries. The first known white settlement in the county was made by Thomas Decker in 1758 near the junction of present-day Decker's Creek and the Monongahela River at Morgantown, but the colony was abandoned after an Indian massacre in 1759. Another settlement at Ice's Ferry along the Cheat River was more successful. It grew into an important shipping and processing center for the iron industry and supported an estimated population of 2,500 at its zenith in the early 1800's.

Monongalia County is the "mother county" of northern West Virginia. The original Monongalia County was larger than the state of Delaware. It was formed in 1776, during the governorship of Patrick Henry, from the Virginia district of West Augusta. The county was named for the Monongahela River, and though spelled differently, both words are taken from the Algonquian Indian tongue and mean 'river of sliding banks.' Twenty counties were later formed from this origi-

nal county, 17 in West Virginia and three in Pennsylvania. In 1790, there were 1,768 people living in Monongalia County. The Monongahela River was used from the time of the earliest settlements to float goods to markets on the Ohio and Mississippi rivers. The first steamboat came to Morgantown in 1826, but navigation of the river by heavy ships was possible only at times of high water. The completion of the lock and dam system in the late 1880's and early 1890's made year-round slackwater navigation of the river a reality.

During the Civil War, the people of Monongalia County were overwhelmingly opposed to secession, and many supported the creation of the new state of West Virginia. Waitman T. Willey (1811-1900) played a large part in the statehood movement and was the first senator from the new state, serving until 1871. Several companies of Union soldiers were raised in the county. Though there were no major battles within the confines of the county's borders, one of the most famous raids occurred at Morgantown in April of 1863, when 2,000 Confederate troops, led by Generals William Jones and John Imboden, invaded Morgantown to gather supplies and horses.

Monongalia County is underlaid by several seams of coal, including the Pittsburgh seam—one of the most valuable coal seams in the world. Coal production began after the Civil War, with two mining establishments producing in the county by 1870. Major commercial mining operations began in the 1880's and reached 11,780,607 tons by 1925. The size of the population of the county in this period reflects this boom, doubling from 24,334 in 1910 to 50,083 in 1930. In 1980, Monongalia County led the state in coal production, mining 12,765,000 tons. Glass has also been a major industry in the county, especially in Morgantown. The population of the county, unlike that of most West Virginia counties, has steadily increased after the 1910-1930 boom period. In 1990, it was 75,509, almost a 20 percent increase over the 1970 population of 63,714.

Morgantown, the county seat, was founded in 1766-68 by Col. Zackquill Morgan on the site of an earlier settlement established in 1758 by Thomas Decker. It became the county seat in 1782 and was named in honor of Morgan and incorporated in 1785. Its population was 1,895 in 1900, 12,127 in 1920, and 25,879 in 1990. Morgantown is the site of the main campus of West Virginia University, the state's largest educational institution. The school is the outgrowth of three earlier academies established in Morgantown—Monongalia Academy (1814), Morgantown Female Academy (1831), and the Woodburn Female Seminary (1858). This property was given to the State of West Virginia in 1867 and, under the provisions of the Morrill Act of 1862, the West Virginia Agricultural College was established. The name was changed to West Virginia University in 1868. The University has an enrollment of over 22,000. In 1988 and 1993, the Mountaineer football teams of Coach Don Nehlen went undefeated, attaining high national ranking. The University's rifle teams have also been successful, winning several national titles in recent years.

Monongalia County Notables
Ralph Albertazzie (1923-). Pilot of Air Force One for three presidents, and a director of W.Va. Department of Commerce.

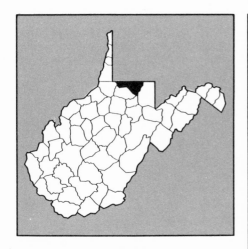

ECONOMIC PROFILE

Poverty status	
(all persons)	20.6%
65 and older	12.3%
Farms/value of farm products sold	390/$2.17 million
Retail sales	$411.79 million
Home ownership	62.1%
Value added by mining	$516.9 million
Median home value	$64,600
Median rent	$297/mo.

Charles Ambler (1876-1937). Noted historian.

Joseph E. Antonini (1932-). Morgantown native, WVU graduate, former President and CEO of Kmart Corporation.

Waitman Barbe (1864-1925). Educator, journalist, and literary critic.

Earl Lemley Core (1902-1984). Historian, educator, and botanist.

William Ellsworth Glasscock (1862-1925). Governor of West Virginia, 1909-1913.

Don Knotts (1924-). Actor and comic.

David Selby (1941-). Actor.

Floyd (Ben) Schwartzwalder (1908-1991). Hall of Fame football coach, all-time winningest coach at Syracuse University. Starred at WVU and was a hero with the famed 82d Airborne Division in World War II.

Israel Charles White (1848-1927). West Virginia's first State Geologist and a geologist of international reputation.

MONONGALIA COUNTY

Land in square miles	363
Total population	75,509
Percentage rural	49.8
Percentage female population	50.4
Percentage African-American population	2.4
Median age	29.2
Birth rate per 1,000 pop.	12.6
Percentage 65 and older	10.9
Median family income	$30,426

Educational attainment

Percent high school graduate or higher	75.4
Percent bachelor's degree or higher	28.1

Monongalia

Bibliography

Callahan, James Morton. *History of the Making of Morgantown, West Virginia: A Type Study in Trans-Appalachian Local History.* Morgantown, Morgantown Printing & Binding Co., 1926. (West Virginia University Studies in History.)

Core, Earl L. *The Monongalia Story: A Bicentennial History.* Parsons, McClain Printing Co., 1974-1984. 5 vols.

Keys, Kevin and Shelly Poe. *Bring on the Mountaineers (100 Years of WVU Football).* Dallas: Taylor Publishing, 1991.

Monongalia Historical Society. *The 175th Anniversary of the Formation of Monongalia County, West Virginia, and Other Relative Historical Data.* [Morgantown] 1954.

Monroe County

West Virginia University's Demonstrational Farm at Willow Bend. (David R. Creel, WVU Photographic Services)

Union, the county seat, was first settled by James Alexander in 1774. The town was granted a charter in 1799. It was named Union because its site had been a meeting place for troops and settlers during the Indian wars of the mid-18th century. Near Union is Rehoboth Church, built in 1786, and said to be the oldest Methodist Church west of the Alleghenies. Union has a population of approximately 600.

Monroe County Notables

Allen Taylor Caperton (1810-1876). United States Senator, 1875-1876.

Ettie Mae Greene (1877-1992). Oldest living American, a Wayside native, died February 26, 1992 leaving four children, 47 grandchildren, and 42 great-grandchildren.

Frank Hereford (1825-1891). United States Senator, 1877-1881.

Andrew S. Rowan (1857-1943). Spanish-American War hero, made famous by Elbert Hubbard's "A Message to Garcia."

Anne Newport Royall (1769-1854). Early journalist considered the first woman reporter and initiator of the interview style of reporting.

Bibliography

Kidd, Barbara. *"The History of Sweet Springs, Monroe County."* West Virginia History, vol. 21 (July 1960) and vol. 22 (October 1960).

Kidd, James R. *"The History of Salt Sulphur Springs, Monroe County."* West Virginia History, vol. 15 (April 1954).

Morton, Oren F. A *History of Monroe County, West Virginia.* Staunton, Va., The McClure Co., Inc., 1916. Reprinted: Baltimore, Md., Regional Publishing Co., 1974.

Motley, Charles B. *Gleanings of Monroe County, West Virginia History.* Radford, Va., Commonwealth Press, 1973.

Monroe County is in the southern tier of counties. Large parts of the county are gently rolling plateaus that contrast greatly with the mountainous ridges of the Alleghenies also existing within the county's boundaries. The area began to be settled by Europeans about 1760. James Moss is generally credited with being the first settler, although little is known about him. The fertile land, well suited for farming, attracted many settlers.

Monroe County was formed from part of Greenbrier County in 1799 and named for James Monroe, fifth President of the United States. The county had a population of 4,188 in 1800, a large number for the time. Indeed, Monroe was until 1850 one of the more heavily populated counties in what was to be West Virginia. Monroe County was from the start an agricultural area. It lies just outside the great coal-producing regions of southern West Virginia. The country's population has been remarkably stable, ranging between 11,000 and 13,000 for the past 100 years.

Monroe County has several mineral springs, some of which were developed into significant tourist attractions, the most noted at Sweet Springs, which attracted many visitors during its great days just before the Civil War. In 1945, the state acquired the property for use as the Andrew S. Rowan Memorial Home for the Aged.

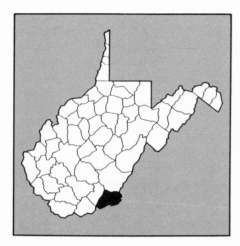

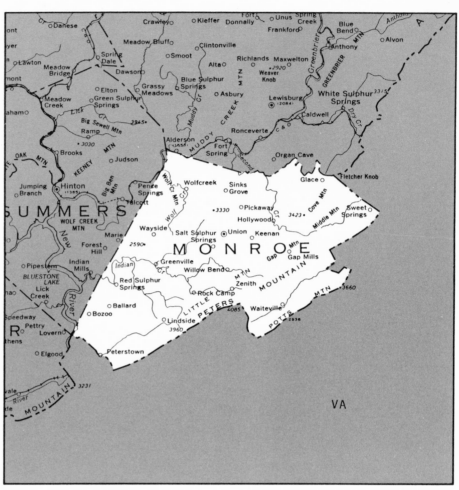

ECONOMIC PROFILE

Poverty status (all persons)	21.0%
65 and older	22.9%
Farms/value of farm products sold	610/$12.38 million
Retail sales	$15.52 million
Home ownership	84.3%
Value added by mining	NA
Median home value	$42,500
Median rent	$151/mo.

MONROE COUNTY

Land in square miles	473
Total population	12,406
Percentage rural	100
Percentage female population	51.5
Percentage African-American population	1.3
Median age	37.5
Birth rate per 1,000 pop.	11.2
Percentage 65 and older	16.9
Median family income	$21,530

Educational attainment

Percent high school graduate or higher	62.1
Percent bachelor's degree or higher	8.0

Morgan County

George Washington loved to vacation in Berkeley Springs because of its naturally warm springs, which gave the town its original name of Bath. The three principal springs and the bathhouses built around them today are part of Berkeley Springs State Park (1925 photograph). (West Virginia and Regional History Collection, WVU Libraries)

Morgan County lies in the Eastern Panhandle in what was once known as the Northern Neck of Virginia. It is located in the Ridge and Valley province of the Appalachian system, and is entirely in the Potomac River basin. In 1747-48, George Washington came to the area to survey the land for Lord Fairfax, an English nobleman who had inherited all of the land drained by the Potomac. The rich limestone soil brought settlers, many of whom entered the area through the Shenandoah River Valley. By 1754, this frontier area was sufficiently populated to warrant the establishment of local government; and Hampshire County, which then included present-day Morgan, Hardy, Grant, and Mineral counties, was formed.

Morgan County residents are proud of the fact that their early property owners included seven members of the Continental Congress (Charles Carroll, Daniel Jenifer, Edward Lloyd, James Mercer, James Smith, George Washington, and James Wilson); three signers of the Declaration of Independence (Carroll, Smith, and Wilson); and three signers of the Constitution (Jenifer, Washington, and Wilson).

In 1820, Morgan County was formed from parts of Berkeley and Hampshire counties and named in honor of General Daniel Morgan, a Revolutionary War leader who was a frequent visitor to Berkeley Springs. The coming of the Baltimore and Ohio Railroad and the Chesapeake and Ohio Canal in the 1830's stimulated trade and brought about the establishment of numerous villages along the Potomac River.

Like most West Virginia counties, Morgan was divided during the Civil War. Though there were no major battles here, the area along the B & O line was considered by both sides to be of critical strategic importance and was heavily defended during most of the war by Union troops. The post-war period was characterized by slow but steady economic development. Improved transportation encouraged the growth of agriculture and sandglass mining, both of which have remained of major importance. The population of the county has grown from 2,500 in 1820 to 7,294 in 1900 and 12,000 in 1990.

Berkeley Springs, the county seat, was established under the name of Bath in 1776 on lands belonging to Lord Fairfax. The curative value of the mineral spring at Berkeley Springs has been known since the days of Indian occupation of the land. Indeed, one historian has speculated that the springs could have been the fabled "Fountain of Youth" for which the Spanish explorer Ponce de Leon searched in vain. The population has remained remarkably constant.

Morgan County Notables
Dr. Lowell Harmison (1939-). Developer of the first implantable heart device, Director of the Maxwell Foundation.

John H. Quick (1861-1925). Author, early conservationist. His "Coolfont" estate is now a popular recreational complex.

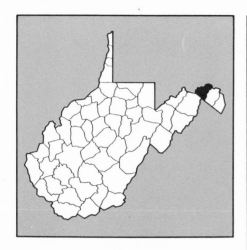

ECONOMIC PROFILE

Poverty status (all persons)	11.0%
65 and older	16.9%
Farms/value of farm products sold	124/$1.26 million
Retail sales	$27.00 million
Home ownership	83.0%
Value added by mining	NA
Median home value	$61,900
Median rent	$217/mo.

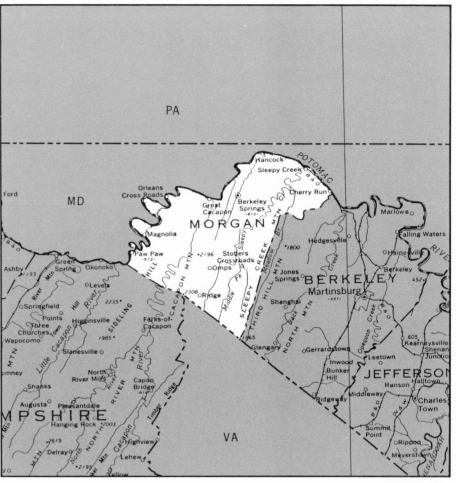

Bibliography

Morgan County Historical and Genealogical Society. *Morgan County, West Virginia, and Its People.* Berkeley Springs, 1981.

Newbraugh, Frederick T. *Warm Springs Echoes: About Berkeley Springs and Morgan County.* (Berkeley Springs) The Morgan Messenger, 1967-1976. 3 vols.

MORGAN COUNTY

Land in square miles	230
Total population	12,128
Percentage rural	100
Percentage female population	51.4
Percentage African-American population	0.8
Median age	38.0
Birth rate per 1,000 pop.	11.6
Percentage 65 and older	16.8
Median family income	$28,252

Educational attainment

Percent high school graduate or higher	64.8
Percent bachelor's degree or higher	11.8

Nicholas County

Carnifex Ferry Civil War Battlefield (L. Victor Haines, WVU Photographic Services)

Nicholas County is located in the central part of the state. The county is drained by the Gauley, Elk, Meadow, Cherry, Williams, and Cranberry rivers. The first white settlers came to the area in about 1785 by way of the Pocahontas trail from the Greenbrier Valley. After 1795, with the danger of Indian raids past, many more families arrived. Nicholas County was formed in 1818 from parts of Kanawha, Greenbrier, and Pocahontas counties. The new county was named for Wilson Nicholas (1761-1820), a former governor of Virginia. In 1820, it had a population of 1,853.

The Civil War saw many skirmishes and one major battle (Carnifex Ferry) in Nicholas County. On September 10, 1861, Union troops led by General William S. Rosecrans attacked Confederate troops commanded by General John B. Floyd. Although the casualties of the Northern troops were high, the battle was considered a Union victory since Floyd's forces were forced to retire. Carnifex Ferry Battlefield Park has been established by the state to commemorate this event. Lumbering has always been one of the major industries of Nicholas County.

Before the railroads were built, logs were cut and floated down the major rivers to mills downstream. In 1899, a branch line of the West Virginia and Pittsburgh Railroad was extended from Camden-on-Gauley to Richwood. Timber operations soon began on the Cranberry and Cherry rivers, and by 1901 Richwood was one of the state's leading lumber towns. The booming lumber business was partially responsible for the sharp increase in population from 11,403 to 20,717 between 1900 and 1920.

As the timber industry began to decline in the 1930's and 1940's, the coal industry gained strength. Production began about 1900 and remained low until the World War II years. By 1950, production reached 3,289,478 tons and continued to rise throughout the 1950's and 1960's, peaking at 6,839,916 tons in 1970. Though production dipped slightly in 1980 to 5,514,000 tons, the coal industry remains important in the county's economy. The recreation industry has grown rapidly in the past two decades. The Summersville Reservoir and part of the Monongahela National Forest are located in the county. Population reached 27,696 in 1950, but declined

to 25,414 in 1960 and 22,552 in 1970. The 1980 census showed a resurgence of population to 28,126, a 24.7 percent increase, but the figure dropped somewhat in the next decade.

Richwood, located on the Cherry River, was incorporated in 1901. It was named for the wealth of natural resources surrounding the town site, especially timber. Thanks to the booming lumber industry, it had a population of 4,331 in 1920. In 1990, the population had dropped to 2,808.

Summersville, the county seat, was established in 1824 and incorporated in 1897. The town was named for Judge Lewis Summers, who introduced the bill creating Nicholas County in the Virginia Assembly. Its population was 279 in 1920 and 2,906 in 1990.

Nicholas County Notables

Stacey Applegate (1977-). International Martial Arts gold medal winner at Budapest in December 1991.

James (Jim) Comstock (1911-1996). Founder of the *West Virginia Hillbilly* and editor of the *West Virginia Heritage Encyclopedia.*

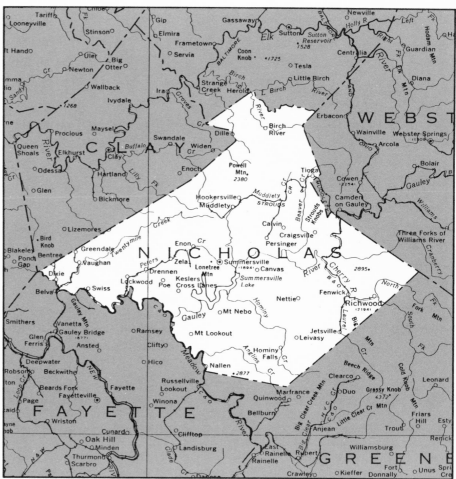

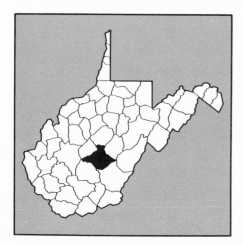

ECONOMIC PROFILE

Poverty status (all persons)	24.4%
65 and older	18.7%
Farms/value of farm products sold	291/$1.90 million
Retail sales	$135.45 million
Home ownership	81.2%
Value added by mining	$153.7
Median home value	$42,300
Median rent	$186/mo.

Nancy Hart (Douglas) (1841-1910). Famous Confederate spy who escaped from Union soldiers at Summersville by shooting her captor.

Russell and Carolee McCauley. Publishers who took over the West Virginia Hillbilly in 1992.

Bibliography

Brown, William Griffee. History of Nicholas County, West Virginia. Richmond, Va., Dietz Press, 1954. Reprinted: Richwood, The News Leader, 1981.

Comstock, Jim and Bronson McClung. *Just For Old Time Sake; A Book From The Past.* Volume One. Richwood, The News Leader, 1949.

NICHOLAS COUNTY

Land in square miles	650
Total population	26,775
Percentage rural	79.3
Percentage female population	51.0
Percentage African-American population	0.0
Median age	34.7
Birth rate per 1,000 pop.	12.5
Percentage 65 and older	13.9
Median family income	$21,390

Educational attainment

Percent high school graduate or higher	61.2
Percent bachelor's degree or higher	8.0

Ohio County

Wheeling Suspension Bridge, an American classic built in 1849. (L. Victor Haines, WVU Photographic Services)

Custom House in Wheeling, birthplace of West Virginia. (L. Victor Haines, WVU Photographic Services)

Ohio County is one of the smallest yet one of the most historically prominent of West Virginia's 55 counties. Nestled between the borders of Pennsylvania and Ohio, its 107 square miles form the heart of the state's slender Northern Panhandle. To its west, the county is flanked by the Ohio River from which it received its name. Ohio is an Indian name meaning "great river."

French explorers under the command of Celoron de Blainville first claimed ownership of the territory in 1749, yet the battle for actual possession was fought several decades later between English settlers and the native Indian population. One of the county's earliest white settlements was established in 1770 by Ebenezer Zane, who staked a claim upon the present site of Wheeling. Over the ensuing decade, Zane's claim became the center of a small community, due in part to the erection of nearby Fort Fincastle in 1774. In 1776, the name was changed to Fort Henry, in honor of Governor Patrick Henry of Virginia. The fort was attacked several times during the Revolution. During the siege in 1782 Betty Zane saved the fort by replenishing its supply of powder. This attack on Fort Henry, September 11-13, 1782—many months after the Battle of Yorktown—was led by 40-50 British Queen's Rangers and 250-300 Indians. It was the last battle of the American Revolution.

Ohio County was officially formed from the district of West Augusta in 1776. The American Revolution slowed traffic into the area, which was besieged by a series of Indian attacks. Rapid growth resumed following the Revolution, so that by the time of the first census in 1790 the county had 5,212 inhabitants. Prosperity continued into the early decades of the 19th century. Due to Wheeling's strategic location on the Ohio River and also to its selection as the terminus of the United States' first east-west roadway, the area soon evolved into a leading center of commerce. An abundance of nearby coal, iron ore, and other natural resources made the area an ideal industrial location.

With its strong ties to northern industry, Ohio County became a hotbed of Unionism during the Civil War. When the state of Virginia joined the Confederacy in 1861, a dissenting Restored Government of Virginia was established with Wheeling as its capital. Wheeling remained the capital city when the new state of West Virginia was formed by act of Congress in 1863, though the seat of government eventually passed to Charleston.

A common misconception is that Wheeling's "Old Custom House" was the first capitol of the state. It was not, but was the capitol of the Restored Government of Virginia, from 1861 to 1863. Remember, Virginia left the Union and joined the Confederate States of America. No matter how Virginians slice it, they joined with a foreign country! But the people of western Virginia opted to stay with the Union, so obviously they were then the Virginia of the United States of America. But their request to be admitted as a separate state was eventually approved and, by President Lincoln's proclamation they were admitted as the state of West Virginia on June 20, 1863. The real first capitol of the new state is the old Linsly Institute building, later known as the Medical Arts Building.

Ohio County's status as the industrial hub of West Virginia continued throughout the later decades of the 19th century and into the 20th. The county's population had reached over 73,000 at the outbreak of World War II. Yet the war itself marked the advent of a gradual decline in inhabitants that has continued to the present. The 1980 census found a population of 61,389, including 43,076 in Wheeling. By 1990, the county total fell to 50,871.

Ohio County boasts the finest municipal park in the nation, Oglebay Park on the outskirts of Wheeling. It's been called "Paradise found," "the model for parks across the nation," and "a country club for the masses." Oglebay's 1500-plus acres offer recreational delights unsurpassed for scope of activity: a hotel with the convenience of a motel, over thirty large family cabins, a 90-acre arboretum, three 18-hole golf courses and thirteen tennis courts, a garden center featuring classic gardens re-created from early 1900's plans, nature trails, outdoor theater, swimming, dancing, and horseback riding. Companion Oglebay Institute boasts the Stifel Fine Arts Center, the historic Mansion Museum, and many other activities. In 1977, the Park opened the gates to the 65-acre Good Children's Zoo, called "West Virginia's Zoo" by *Wonderful West Virginia Magazine.* This amazing zoo is home to more than 200 different animals including otters, red wolves, and bison. The zoo

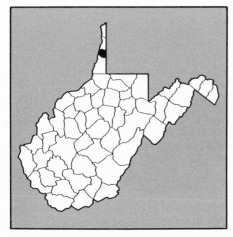

ECONOMIC PROFILE

Poverty status	
(all persons)	15.0%
65 and older	15.8%
Farms/value of farm products sold	142/$1.85 million
Retail sales	$309.98 million
Home ownership	66.7%
Value added by mining	NA
Median home value	$48,800
Median rent	$209/mo.

has in a captive breeding program several of the red wolves, of which fewer than 150 remain in the world.

Oglebay boasts much more, including the Festival of Lights (over a million lights) at Christmas time (actually November to February) and the Festival of Flowers through much of the rest of the year. People come from all over the US and Canada to see these extravaganzas.

Wheeling was known alternately as *Zanesburg* and *Weelin* (an Indian word meaning place of the skull) in its early years. The city was incorporated in 1806 and officially chartered by the Virginia Assembly in 1836. With a population in excess of 8,000, by the latter year the city had become a robust industrial center embracing no fewer than ten glass and glassware manufacturers, four iron foundries, and many other factories. As the western terminus of both the national roadway and eventually the B & O

OHIO COUNTY

Land in square miles	107
Total population	50,871
Percentage rural	20.2
Percentage female population	53.5
Percentage African-American population	3.3
Median age	37.7
Birth rate per 1,000 pop.	12.5
Percentage 65 and older	18.9
Median family income	$30,037

Educational attainment

Percent high school graduate or higher	75.1
Percent bachelor's degree or higher	18.4

Ohio

"Cascading Waters" - Free show presented on Oglebay's Schenk Lake every Spring and Fall.

The Mansion Museum (built in 1835).

Railroad, the city was an important east-west crossroad. A bridge built over the Ohio River by the city in 1849 was, at the time, the longest suspension bridge in the world, with a 1,010-foot span.

A variety of cultural endeavors followed closely on the heels of the city's industrial and technological advances. A library, a theater, and a variety of schools and academies were all established by the mid-19th century. The city can also boast a vigorous concert life and singing society tradition thanks to its renowned Wheeling Symphony. Wheeling's musical reputation is well known to all listeners of Radio Station WWVA, which since its inception has made the city a center of country music. The city is the home of Wheeling Jesuit University and West Virginia Northern Community College. Also located in Wheeling are two of the region's best-known preparatory schools— Linsly Institute and Mount de Chantal Visitation Academy. Oglebay Park is regarded as one of the finest educational and recreational centers in the country.

Wheeling has consistently been rated in the top ten "Best Places to Live" by *Places Rated Almanac,* published by Rand McNally (e.g., the 1992 listing placed Wheeling second in the country).

West Liberty, a town of 1,434 in 1990, carries the distinction of being the first chartered town in the Ohio Valley (1787). Originally known as Black's Cabin after the site of Ohio County's first judicial meeting, the town also served as the county seat between 1777-97. West Liberty is perhaps best known today as the site of West Liberty State College whose lineage extends back to the founding of West Liberty Academy in 1837.

Ohio County Notables

George W. Atkinson (1845-1925). Governor of West Virginia, 1897- 1901.

Stuart Bloch (1933-). Wheeling executive and President of the US Golf Association.

Jesse Cail Burkett (1868-1942?). Hall of Fame major league baseball player with a lifetime batting average of .342.

Brian Caveney (1970-). WVU medical student chosen as one of the top 20 scholars in the nation by USA Today in 1991, already having accomplished important medical research, particularly on Reyes Syndrome.

Lydia Boggs Shepherd Cruger (1765-1867). Frontierswoman and socialite prominent in much of two centuries.

Rebecca Harding Davis (1831-1910). Novelist and short story writer.

Jack Glasscock (1867?-1940?). Wheeling Island neighbor of Burkett (see above) who also made the major leagues (shortstop, 1879-1895).

Harry Hamm (1923-1991). Longtime Wheeling newspaper editor who authored the WHEELING 2000 plan for the city's future.

Lester C. Hess, Jr. (1940-). National leader of the Fraternal Order of Elks in 1992.

Alberta Pierson Hannum (1906-1985). Novelist and historian.

Simon P. Hullihen (1810-1857). Wheeling dentist, the "Father of Oral Surgery."

Ohio

James D. Moffat (1846-1915). General Moderator of the Presbyterian Church, president of Washington and Jefferson College, 1881-1914, longer than any other.

Earl William Oglebay (1849-1926). Wealthy businessman who left his estate, Waddington, to the city of Wheeling—now nationally-renowned Oglebay Park.

Fritzi Stifel Quarrier (1904-1985). Won state amateur title ten times, first woman in the W.Va. Hall of Fame.

Jesse Lee Reno (1823-1862). Union Army major general killed in the battle of South Mountain, Maryland. Reno, Nevada was named for him.

Most Rev. Bernard W. Schmitt (1928-). Wheeling native who became Bishop of the Wheeling and Charleston Dioceses of the Catholic Church in 1989.

Eleanor Steber (1914-). World renowned opera star.

William Weiss (1879-1942). Founded Sterling Drug Company, once the world's largest manufacturer of proprietary remedies, and the American Home Products Company.

Rachael Worby - Conductor of the Wheeling Symphony and first lady of Gov. Gaston Caperton (1988-1997).

Other Notables . . .

Boury Brothers, Sally Carroll, Louis Corson, Leland Devore, Alexander Glass, Russell B. Goodwin, Virginia Jones Harper, Dr. A. Earl Hennen, Chuck Howley, Chester D. Hubbard, Chester R. Hubbard, James Kindelberger, John Kirkland, George Kossuth, Howard Long, Ray Montgomery, Joseph Ray, Walter P. Reuther, Paul Rickards, Jules Rivlin, Dr. Abraham Robertson, Constance Cornell Stuart, Nancy King Stumpp, Sue Vail, Lawrence Washington, and Chickie Williams.

Bibliography

Featherling, Doug. *Wheeling, An Illustrated History.* Woodland Hills, Calif., Windsor Publications, 1983.

Harper, Virginia Jones. Time Steals Softly. Pittsburgh, Pa: Dorrance and Co., 1992.

Newton, J. H., G. G. Nichols, and A. G. Sprankle. *History of the Panhandle: Being Historical Collections of the Counties of Ohio, Brooke, Marshall, and Hancock, West Virginia.* Wheeling, J. A. Caldwell, 1879. Reprinted: Evansville, Ind., Unigraphic, Inc., 1973.

Wavra, Grace. *The First Families of West Virginia.* Huntington, WV: University Editions, 1990.

Wingerter, Charles A., ed. *History of Greater Wheeling and Vicinity, A Chronicle of Progress and a Narrative Account of the Industries, Institutions and People of the City and Tributary Territory.* Chicago, Ill., The Lewis Publishing Co., 1912. 2 vols.

Pendleton County

Above: Seneca Rocks (L. Victor Haines, WVU Photographic Services)

Right: Spruce Knob, highest point in West Virginia at 4,860 feet above sea level. (Gerald S. Ratliff, West Virginia Department of Commerce)

Pendleton County is located in the eastern part of the state. The county is trisected by three great mountain ridges running in a northeasterly direction. Spruce Knob, part of the westernmost ridge, is the highest point in West Virginia, 4,860 feet. Located between these three ridges are two valleys in which the tributaries of the South Branch of the Potomac —the North and South Forks—flow and in which most of the initial settlements were made.

By the mid-1740's there were a number of settlers living along the South Branch tributaries, many of them Germans. During the French and Indian War, these scattered settlements were subjected to several Indian raids. In 1758, a party of about 40 Indians, led by the Delaware Chief Killbuck, attacked Fort Upper Tract and Fort Seybert and massacred most of their white inhabitants. The last Indian raid into the county took place in 1781.

Pendleton County was created in 1788 from parts of Augusta, Hardy, and Rockingham counties. It was named for Edmund Pendleton (1721-1803), a distinguished statesman and jurist of Virginia. In 1790, its population was 2,452; by 1860, its population was 6,164. Pendleton County has always been a predominantly agricultural area, with industrial development hampered by the rugged terrain and the lack of railroads. Besides livestock and other agricultural products, a considerable amount of unfinished lumber is produced and trucked to mills in other areas. The population of the county peaked at 10,884 in 1940, then declined to 7,031 in 1970. The 1990 census showed a 12.5 percent increase.

A sizeable part of Pendleton County is taken up by public lands. The Shenandoah National Forest is located in the eastern section of the county and the Monongahela Na-

tional Forest, which includes Spruce Knob, is located in the western section. Also located in the county are Seneca Rocks, the Smoke Hole and Seneca Caverns, and other significant limestone caves. The county includes some of the most beautiful scenery in the state. Tourism is one of the major industries and may be expected to grow in importance.

Franklin, the county seat, was chartered in 1794 and named Franksford for Francis Evick, one of the county's first settlers. The town was later renamed in honor of Benjamin Franklin. Its population was 200 in 1910 and 914 in 1990. It is the only municipality in the county.

Pendleton County Notables
General John C. Bond (1880-1950). Served in Spanish-American War and World War I, and as adjutant general and auditor of the state.

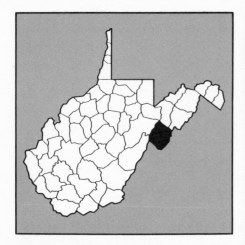

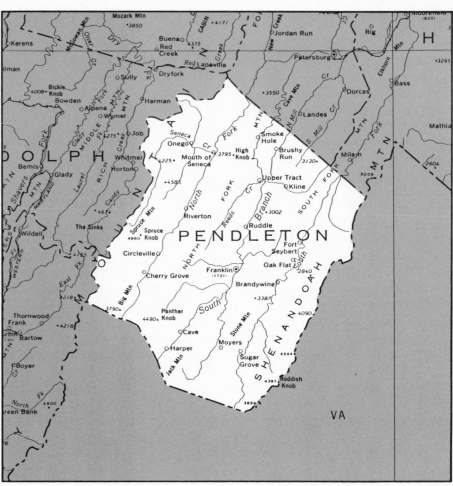

ECONOMIC PROFILE

Poverty status (all persons)	17.0%
65 and older	29.3%
Farms/value of farm products sold	561/$34.87 million
Retail sales	$18.01 million
Home ownership	79.3%
Value added by mining	NA
Median home value	$51,600
Median rent	$190/mo.

Larkins Bruce Bowers (1877-1937). Minister, educator, and president of Kansas Wesleyan College; died in a Kansas auto accident at age 60.

Howard Hill Johnson (1846-1913). Blind crusader who founded the West Virginia Schools for The Deaf and The Blind.

Joseph McClure (1838-1915). Confederate soldier who became "Cattle King of West Virginia" with some 10,000 acres of grazing land.

Bibliography

Boggs, Elsie Byrd. *A History of Franklin, the County Seat of Pendleton County, West Virginia.* Staunton, Va., McClure Printing Co., 1960.

Morton, Oren F. A *History of Pendleton County, West Virginia.* Franklin, The Author, 1910. Reprinted: Baltimore, Md., Regional Publishing Co., 1974.

Writers' Program. West Virginia. *The Smoke Hole and Its People.* Revised edition. Huntington (1941?) (Folk Studies, No. 3.)

PENDLETON COUNTY

Land in square miles	698
Total population	8,054
Percentage rural	100
Percentage female population	50.1
Percentage African-American population	2.1
Median age	36.6
Birth rate per 1,000 pop.	11.4
Percentage 65 and older	17.3
Median family income	$22,500

Educational attainment

Percent high school graduate or higher	60.6
Percent bachelor's degree or higher	8.2

Pleasants County

Pleasants County Courthouse at Saint Marys, first settled in 1790. (L. Victor Haines, WVU Photographic Services)

Pleasants County, one of the smallest of West Virginia's counties, lies by the Ohio River in the western part of the state. The county is divided into two nearly equal portions by Middle Island Creek. Within its borders, both fertile bottom land and the highlands of the Appalachian foothills can be found. The area's first recorded permanent settlement was made by a pair of French brothers, Isaac and Jacob LaRue in 1790. They had been awarded a grant of land in return for their service to the American cause during the Revolutionary War. Pleasants County was formed from three other counties, Wood, Tyler, and Ritchie, in 1851. It was named after James Pleasants (1769-1836), Governor of Virginia from 1822 to 1825. The population in 1860 was 2,945.

Agriculture and timber were for many years the major sources of income. These were supplanted starting in the 1890's by oil and gas. The oil fields proved to be extremely produc-tive and brought great wealth to the area. While the boom period lasted less than 20 years, oil and gas are still significant sources of revenue. The majority of the county's population (7,546 in 1990) now find employment in nearby industries and in agriculture.

St. Marys, the county seat, is located on the banks of the Ohio. The town was founded by Alexander Creel in 1849. According to legend, Creel was traveling by steamboat down the Ohio when he beheld a vision of the Virgin Mary who told him that a city founded at the joining of the Ohio River and Middle Island Creek would be happy and prosperous. Creel bought the land, marked off the streets for his city, and named it in honor of the Virgin Mary. The town had a population of 2,148 in 1990.

Willow Island was the scene of a ter-rible tragedy on April 27, 1978-51 workers fell 168 feet to their deaths in scaffolding collapse at the Pleasants Power Plant.

Pleasants County Notables

Charles H. Ambler (1876-1957). Educator, historian, and member of the House of Delegates.

Hiram Carpenter (1880-1967). Known as "The Potato King," he raised them on islands in the Ohio River. He ran ferries at St. Mary's and helped build the "Hi Carpenter Bridge."

Brooks Fleming Ellis (1897-1977). Eminent geologist and educator noted for his pioneering work in pa-leontology.

Bibliography

Fleming, Dan B. *From A Riverbank: Sketches from Pleasants County His-tory.* Edited by Dan B. Fleming, Jr. [n.p.] Pleasants County Historical Association, 1976.

Pemberton, Robert L. *A History of Pleasants County, West Virginia.* St. Marys, West Virginia: The Oracle Press, 1929.

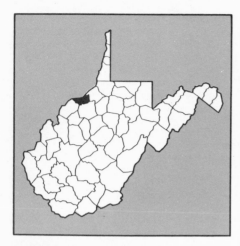

ECONOMIC PROFILE

Poverty status	
(all persons)	19.4%
65 and older	16.7%
Farms/value of farm products sold	89/$536,000
Retail sales	$28.89 million
Home ownership	79.6%
Value added by mining	NA
Median home value	$51,100
Median rent	$178/mo.

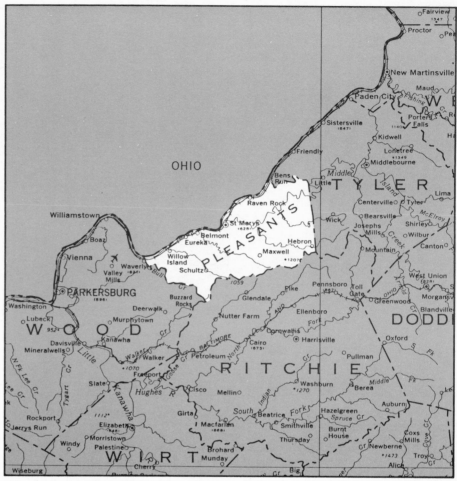

PLEASANTS COUNTY

Land in square miles	131
Total population	7,546
Percentage rural	100
Percentage female population	51.4
Percentage African-American population	0.2
Median age	34.9
Birth rate per 1,000 pop.	13.5
Percentage 65 and older	14.5
Median family income	$26,110

Educational attainment

Percent high school graduate or higher	68.7
Percent bachelor's degree or higher	8.5

Pocahontas County

Radio telescopes, which enable astronomers to collect and measure radio waves to find out more about the universe, are located in Deer Creek Valley near Green Bank, with nearby mountains providing a natural shield against harmful radio interference. (Associated Universities, Inc,)

Pocahontas County is located in the east-central part of the state. The terrain is rugged and mountainous, with a number of peaks reaching 4,500 feet. The county has been called the "birthplace of rivers" because eight rivers have their headwaters there—the Greenbrier, Shaver's Fork of the Cheat, the Tygart Valley, the Williams, the Cherry, the Cranberry, the Gauley, and the Elk.

The first known white settlers in the area were Jacob Marlin and Stephen Sewell, who settled along the Greenbrier River in 1749. Sewell was killed by Indians, but Marlin survived and established one of the first permanent settlements west of the Allegheny Mountains. During the French and Indian War (1755-63), Fort Greenbrier was built at Marlin's settlement to guard it from Indian at-

tacks. The last Indian raid in this area was in 1786.

By 1821, the population of the area had grown enough to warrant the creation of Pocahontas County from parts of Bath (Virginia), Randolph, and Pendleton counties. The county was named for the Indian princess who saved the life of Captain John Smith. In 1830, the population of the county was 3,422. During the Civil War the county was the site of the battle of Droop Mountain. On November 6, 1863, the Union general W. W. Averell and his army defeated a Confederate army led by General John Echols. This was the most extensive conflict fought wholly within the state, with over 9,000 troops engaged in combat. It was also one of the most decisive battles since it effectively ended Southern resistance in the state. The

battlefield site, located near Hillsboro, was acquired by the state in 1929 and made into a state park.

When the virgin forests of the county were harvested in the late 1800's and early 1900's, the wood was floated down the Greenbrier River or shipped on the railways which connected the county to the Chesapeake and Ohio mainline. Tanneries were established at Durbin and Marlinton, and by 1920 the population of the county had grown to 15,002—an all-time high. In the 1920's and 1930's the federal government began buying land for the Monongahela National Forest, and today more than half of the county's land is publicly owned. In 1970, the population of the county dipped to 8,870, but has since increased.

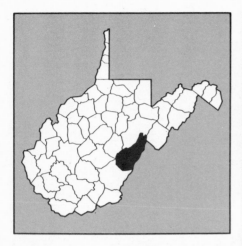

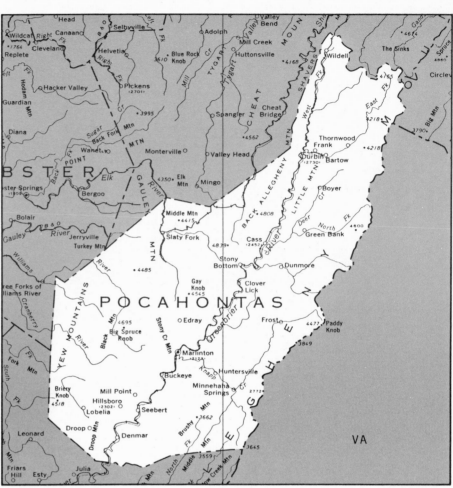

ECONOMIC PROFILE

Poverty status (all persons)	21.2%
65 and older	23.9%
Farms/value of farm products sold	379/$4.91 million
Retail sales	$32.62 million
Home ownership	79.4%
Value added by mining	NA
Median home value	$42,000
Median rent	$177/mo.

Pocahontas County offers many opportunities for recreation. Besides Monongahela National Forest, there are several state-owned parks, forests, and historic sites—Watoga State Park (the oldest and largest state park), Beartown State Park, Droop Mountain Battlefield Park, Seneca State Forest, Calvin W. Price State Forest, and the Cass Scenic Railroad. The Pearl S. Buck Museum, located in Hillsboro, commemorates the life and career of this world-famous author.

Marlinton, the county seat, is located on the Greenbrier River. It was settled in 1749 by Jacob Marlin and was first known as Marlin's Bottom. The name was changed to Marlinton in 1887. In 1891, the county seat was moved from Huntersville to Marlinton. In 1910, the town had a population of 1,045; in 1990 it was 1,148.

Pocahontas County Notables
Bruce Bosley (1933-1995). All-American football player at WVU who went

POCAHONTAS COUNTY

Land in square miles	942
Total population	9,008
Percentage rural	100
Percentage female population	50.2
Percentage African-American population	0.8
Median age	38.5
Birth rate per 1,000 pop.	13.5
Percentage 65 and older	18.8
Median family income	$20,595

Educational attainment

Percent high school graduate or higher	60.6
Percent bachelor's degree or higher	9.7

Pocahontas

on to an all-pro career with San Francisco and Atlanta in the NFL.

Pearl S. Buck (1892-1973). Author and Nobel Prize winner.

James E. A. Gibbs (1829-1902). Invented new type sewing machine in the 1850's, served in the Confederate Army.

John Snowden Kellison (1886-1971). Wesleyan (football player) Canton Bulldogs player and coach, sports writer,.

Bibliography

McNeill, George D. *Tales of Pocahontas County.* Marlinton 1959.

Pocahontas County Historical Society, Inc. *History of Pocahontas County, West Virginia 1981: Birthplace of Rivers.* Marlinton, 1981.

Price, William T. *Historical Sketches of Pocahontas County, West Virginia.* Marlinton, Price Brothers, 1901.

Preston County

Earth tracking station of Communications Satellite Corporation at Etam. (David R. Creel, WVU Photographic Services)

Preston County is located in the north-central part of the state. Most of the county is drained by the Cheat River, though the Youghiogheny River rises in the southeastern corner of the county near the Maryland border. It is an area characterized by high rolling uplands. The first known permanent settler to arrive in Preston was Thomas Butler, in 1766. Population was sparse for many years because transportation was poor and much of the land difficult to farm.

Preston County was formed in 1818 from Monongalia County and was named in honor of James Peyton Preston, Governor of Virginia from 1816-1818. In 1820 it had a population of 3,422. In the 1850's the Baltimore and Ohio Railroad was completed through Preston County, link-

ing it with Baltimore to the east and Wheeling to the west. Though at first the railroad passed through near wilderness, villages sprang up along the route. Coal production in Preston County began in the years following the Civil War, and by 1920 it had reached 1,909,128 tons. The lumber industry experienced a boom in this period as well, and by 1920 the population of the county had reached 27,996. Population declined considerably for several decades but started to increase in recent years. Coal mining has remained an important source of income and employment. Production for 1983 was 2.6 million tons.

Preston County was the site of one of the best-known social experiments of the 1930's, When the federal government attempted to alleviate the ef-

fects of the Depression on coal miners and their families by establishing a model homestead project at Arthurdale. The project was of special interest to Eleanor Roosevelt, who made frequent visits to the community. Because of Mrs. Roosevelt's involvement, Arthurdale received much publicity and was the center of both interest and controversy. Federal support was withdrawn at the outset of the Second World War, and the buildings are now privately owned.

Kingwood, the county seat, was established in 1811 and incorporated in 1853. It was named for the unusual number of tall and stately trees growing in the area at the time. Its population was 3,243 in 1990.

Terra Alta, formerly Green Glades, Cranberry Summit, and Portland, was incorporated in 1890. It takes its present name from the Latin words for "high land." Its population was 1,713 in 1990.

Preston County Notables

Izetta Jewel Brown (1884-1978). Political pioneer, first woman to run for the US Senate from south of the Mason-Dixon Line (lost in primary to Senator Neely in 1922).

William G. Brown, Sr. (1800-1884) and Jr. (1856-1916). Both served in the US House of Representatives.

William G. Conley (1866-1940). Governor of West Virginia, 1929-1933.

William M. Dawson (1853-1916). Governor of West Virginia, 1905-1909.

John Marshall Hagans (1838-1900). Member of the US House of Representatives and a fine jurist.

Mahlon Loomis (1826-1886). Dentist and inventor who developed the first wireless communications system in the 1860's.

Rex Elwood Pyles (1910-1982). Born in Independence in this county, starred in football and basketball at Shinnston High School and Glenville State College. NAIA Hall of Fame coach.

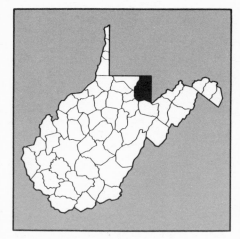

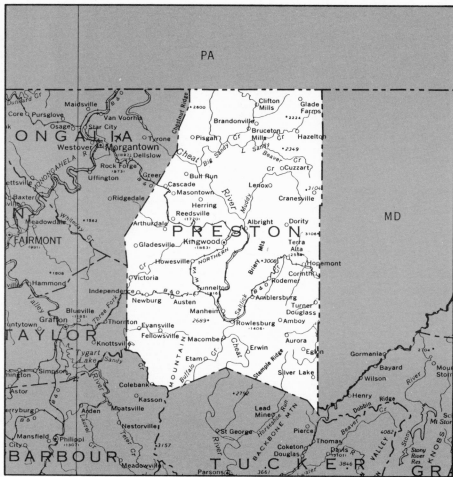

ECONOMIC PROFILE

Poverty status (all persons)	18.9%
65 and older	20.0%
Farms/value of farm products sold	714/$10.28 million
Retail sales	$92.57 million
Home ownership	81.3%
Value added by mining	$62.9 million
Median home value	$44,200
Median rent	$176/mo.

Bibliography

Morton, Oren F. *A History of Preston County, West Virginia.* Kingwood, The Journal Publishing Co., 1914. 2 vols.

Preston County Historical Society. *Preston County, West Virginia, History 1979.* Kingwood, 1979.

Teets, Bob. *West Virginia UFOs: Close Encounters in the Mountain State.* Terra Alta: Headline Books, 1994.

Teets, Jo Ann Sereno. *From This Green Glade: A History of Terra Alta, West Virginia.* Terra Alta, 1978.

PRESTON COUNTY

Land in square miles	651
Total population	29,037
Percentage rural	90.6
Percentage female population	50.7
Percentage African-American population	0.3
Median age	34.5
Birth rate per 1,000 pop.	11.8
Percentage 65 and older	14.0
Median family income	$23,222

Educational attainment

Percent high school graduate or higher	62.7
Percent bachelor's degree or higher	8.3

Putnam County

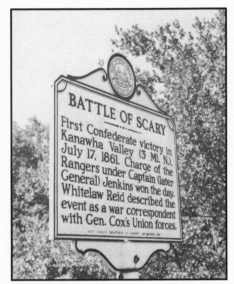

This is the site of the first major Civil War skirmish in the Kanawha Valley. (L. Victor Haines WVU Photographic Services)

Putnam County lies in the Kanawha River valley, in the southwestern part of West Virginia. Within the county can be found fertile river valley land and ranges of high hills. While the region was known to early explorers, permanent settlement did not begin until about 1800. For many decades, settlements were confined largely to the bottom lands of the Kanawha and its tributaries.

Putnam County was created in 1848 from parts of Cabell, Kanawha, and Mason counties and named after Israel Putnam, the Revolutionary War hero. The county had a population of approximately 5,000 at the time of its establishment. Agriculture was for many years the only significant source of income. There were no major towns, and the population grew very slowly. However, an increasingly important

coal industry began to develop in the 1880's. Coal production, 135,100 tons in 1888, grew to over 300,000 tons by 1905, and to over 500,000 tons by 1911.

The new employment opportunities attracted settlers, and the county's population increased from 11,375 in 1880 to 18,587 in 1910. Coal production began to decline rapidly after 1940 and is now of little significance. However, the slack was more than taken up by the many employment opportunities, especially in the chemical industry, in the Kanawha Valley. Putnam is one of the few counties in the state that has seen a steady growth in population in every census since 1930, serving as a bedroom community for Charleston and Huntington, the state's largest cities.

Winfield, laid out in 1848, is the county seat. The town was named for General

Winfield Scott, hero of the Mexican War. It is located on the Kanawha River.

Nitro is the county's largest city. The town's name came from the federal munitions plant built there towards the end of World War I. The town sprang up to house the workers at this plant. Near Nitro is the world's largest coal-burning power plant, the John E. Amos facility on the Great Kanawha River. Nitro had a population of 6,851 in 1980.

Putnam County Notables

Virginia Mae Brown (1923-   ). West Virginia's first woman insurance commissioner; first woman ever appointed to the Interstate Commerce Commission (1964).

Selva "Lou" Lewis Burdette (1927-   ). Nitro High School graduate who went directly from a local industrial

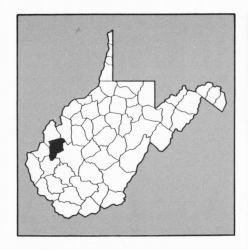

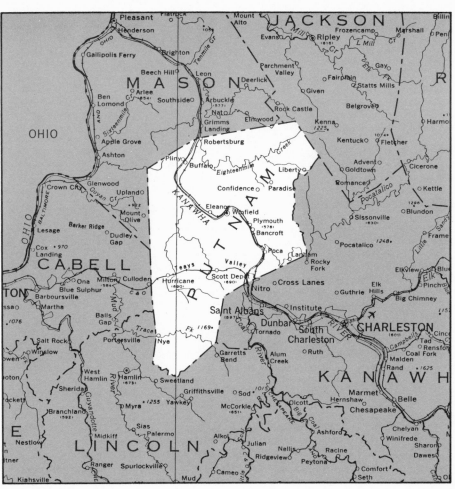

ECONOMIC PROFILE

Poverty status	
(all persons)	12.0%
65 and older	18.5%
Farms/value of farm products sold	470/$2.46 million
Retail sales	$175.58 million
Home ownership	83.3%
Value added by mining	NA
Median home value	$62,700
Median rent	$265/mo.

baseball league to the majors to become one of the all-time great right-hand pitchers.

William Hope "Coin" Harvey (1851-1936). Lawyer, economist, and author whose book, *Coin's Financial School,* sold over one million copies in the 1890's.

Bibliography

"Hardesty's Putnam County." *West Virginia Heritage Encyclopedia.* Supplemental Series, vol. 1.

History of Buffalo, Putnam County, West Virginia. Point Pleasant, Mattox Printing Service, 1976.

Hunter, Ivan N. *The Poca-Raymond City Story.* [St. Albans] Upper Vandalia Historical Society, 1981.

Wintz, William D., and Ivan N. Hunter. *The History of Putnam County.* [St. Albans] Upper Vandalia Historical Society, 1967.

PUTNAM COUNTY

Land in square miles	346
Total population	42,835
Percentage rural	48.1
Percentage female population	51.0
Percentage African-American population	0.3
Median age	34.2
Birth rate per 1,000 pop.	12.7
Percentage 65 and older	11.0
Median family income	$31,448

Educational attainment

Percent high school graduate or higher	73.8
Percent bachelor's degree or higher	13.3

Raleigh County

Grandview State Park near Beckley. (Gerald S. Ratliff, West Virginia Department of Commerce)

Raleigh County is located in the south-central part of the state. Most of the land is rough and hilly, but a section in the central part of the county is an upland plateau with rolling and flat terrain. The county lies in the drainage basin of the New, Guyandotte, and Coal rivers.

The lack of roads and navigable streams in the Raleigh area delayed its settlement until the first half of the 19th century. In 1837, General Alfred Beckley brought his family from Pittsburgh into the plateau area and built a home which he aptly called "Wildwood." The home, restored, was in 1971 placed on the National Register of Historic Places and is now a museum. The rich and productive soil of the plateau region attracted settlers, and soon there were several pioneer families living in the area. These pioneer settlements formed the basis for the development of the modern town of Beckley.

In 1850 this upland area was sufficiently populated to warrant the creation of a new county, and in that year the Virginia legislature passed an act forming Raleigh County from Fayette County. The county was named in honor of Sir Walter Raleigh and in 1850 had a population of 1,765.

Soon after the Civil War, extensive lumbering operations commenced on the more accessible tracts of land. Much of the land where the city of Beckley now stands was once a huge pine forest and there were valuable hardwoods in the other sections of the county. Since agriculture was not practical on the steep mountain slopes and narrow valleys of much of the county, speculators from the northeastern cities were able to acquire these uplands cheaply and in large tracts. Timber, and later coal, came from these extensive tracts. The timber industry was partially responsible for the county's first economic boom. In the 20-year period from 1880 to 1900 the population increased from 7,367 to 12,436.

In 1873, the Chesapeake and Ohio Railroad completed a line along the New River on the eastern border of the county. Later, the C & O constructed a branch line through the mid-section of the county, opening up the New River Coal Field in the eastern part of the county. Later, in 1909, the Virginian Railway opened up a line north of the C & O. Coal mining dominated the economy of the county from 1900 to 1950 and was largely responsible for the growth in population from 12,436 in 1900 to 96,273 in 1950.

Beckley, a small town of 342 people in 1900, grew to a city of 4,149 by 1920 and was acclaimed the "Smokeless Coal Capital of the World." Numerous coal towns sprang up across the county along the railroads near the major coal mines. Tams, Fireco, Eccles, Glen White, and Stone Coal are some of these boom towns that are still in existence. At Eccles, along the Virginian Railway, a major explosion killed 183 men at a mine in 1914. Coal production went from 76,563 tons in 1900 to 2,853,448 tons in 1910 and to a peak of 15,484,171 tons in 1950. In 1950, the coal mines of the county employed 13,549 men.

The coal boom came to a halt in the 1950's. The combination of a slack coal market and increasing mechanization squeezed many of the marginal mines out of existence. Coal production dropped to 7,124,177 tons in 1960 and 6,838,000 tons in 1980. Population dropped along with coal production, hitting a modern low of 70,080 in 1970. In the 1970's, the people of Raleigh County responded to the economic slump by diversifying their economy. The manufacturing, retail, and other service industries have expanded rapidly and have brought a more broad-based economy to the county. Population increased by 23.9 percent during the decade 1970-1980.

This county has a claim as the glass marbles capital of the world. Naoma native Ray Jarrell won the National Marbles Championship and led a United States team to victory over England in the 1970s. In 1980, a team from the area won the national team title. In 1983, two West Virginia boys from Mountainview battled it out for the national championship as Kerry Acord beat Carmel Burnside. Some 14 national marbles champs have hailed from West Virginia.

Raleigh is the home of Grandview State Park, host to two West Virginia historical dramas each summer. Flat Top is the location of the annual Lilly Family Reunion, one of the country's largest.

Beckley, the county seat, was named for John Beckley, first clerk of the United States Congress, and first Librarian of Congress. The town had a population of 342 in 1900, but began to grow very rapidly with the devel-

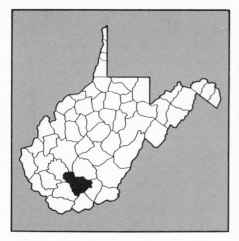

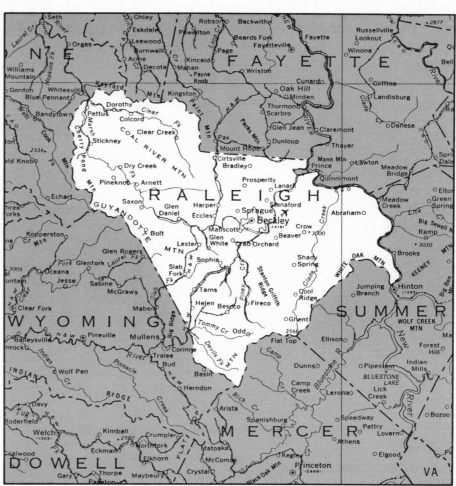

ECONOMIC PROFILE

Poverty status	
(all persons)	19.9%
65 and older	12.5%
Farms/value of farm products sold	260/$1.78 million
Retail sales	$464.64 million
Home ownership	75.5%
Value added by mining	$224.5 million
Median home value	$44,100
Median rent	$218/mo.

opment of the coal industry, of which it became a center. In 1920, Beckley had a population of over 4,000 and in 1990 was a city of 18,296.

Raleigh County Notables

Robert Carlyle Byrd (1918-). A United States Senator since 1958, he has served as both the Majority and Minority Leader.

Harley M. Kilgore (1893-1956). United States Senator from West Virginia, 1941-1956.

Clarence W. Meadows (1904-1961). Governor of West Virginia, 1945-1949.

Chris Sarandon (1942-). Actor.

Tommy Small (1970-). Sophia native who was the world superwelterweight champion in 1993.

Hulett C. Smith (1918-). Governor of West Virginia, 1965-1969.

Harry Adams Stansbury (1891-1966). Sports star and coach at West Virginia Wesleyan, then athletic director at WVU, 1917-1938.

RALEIGH COUNTY

Land in square miles	608
Total population	76,819
Percentage rural	72.4
Percentage female population	52.9
Percentage African-American population	7.7
Median age	36.1
Birth rate per 1,000 pop.	11.6
Percentage 65 and older	15.3
Median family income	$24,391

Educational attainment

Percent high school graduate or higher	63.2
Percent bachelor's degree or higher	10.7

Bibliography

Hedrick, Charles B., comp. *Memoirs of Raleigh County, Historical and Biographical*. Beckley, Wood Printing Co., 1932.

Randolph County

Randolph County Courthouse at Elkins.

Fall Forest Festival at Elkins.

Randolph County is located in the east-central part of the state and is the largest county in the state. The terrain is mountainous, the highest point being Snyder Knob with an elevation of 4,730 feet. The county is drained by the Elk, Tygart, Buckhannon, Middle Fork, and Cheat rivers.

The first known white settlers in Randolph County were Robert Files and David Tygart and their families, who settled along the Tygart Valley River in about 1753. Files and his family were killed by Indians in 1755; Tygart, warned of the raid, retreated to the east. It was not until 1772 that permanent settlements were made in the county. Randolph County was formed in 1787 from Harrison County and at first included all of present-day Tucker County, and part of Barbour, Upshur, Pocahontas, and Webster counties. It was named for Edmund Jennings Randolph, Governor of Virginia, 1786-1788. In 1790 it had a population of 951.

Much of the early fighting in the Civil War in West Virginia took place in Randolph County. On July 11, 1861, the battle of Rich Mountain was fought five miles west of Beverly between the Union forces, led by General George B. McClellan, and the Confederate forces, led by General Robert S. Garnett. The battle resulted in an overwhelming Union victory, and it left Union forces in complete control of the Monongahela Valley and an important section of the Baltimore and Ohio Railroad.

Randolph County's economy was based almost entirely on agriculture until 1889, when the West Virginia Central and Pittsburgh Railway Company, headed by Henry G. Davis and Stephen B. Elkins, completed a line from Elkins in Randolph County to Piedmont in Mineral County. This line linked the county with the mainline of the Baltimore and Ohio Railroad and spurred the exploitation of the area's abundant timber and coal resources.

Coal production began in 1900, with 76,563 tons produced in that year. Production rose to 884,735 tons in 1920, and in 1980 it reached 1,237,000 tons. In the two decades between 1890 and 1910, the population of the county more than doubled, jumping from 11,633 in 1890 to 26,028 in 1910. It peaked in 1950 at 30,558, dipped to 24,596 in 1970, and then began to increase again to over 27,000 in 1990.

Randolph County is renowned for the Mountain State Forest Festival, which is held each year at Elkins. The festival, which attracts visitors from across the nation, is dedicated to the preservation of the state's forest lands. The Kumbrabow State Forest, as well as part of the Monongahela National Forest, are located in the county.

Elkins, the county seat, was originally known as Leadville. It was renamed in 1890 in honor of Senator Stephen B. Elkins. Its population was 6,788 in 1920 and 7,420 in 1990. Davis and Elkins College, located in Elkins, was founded in 1904 by the Presbyterian Church with aid from Henry Davis and Stephen Elkins. This private institution has an enrollment of approximately 1,000. In 1992, Davis and Elkins dedicated a new four-level, $7 million Booth Library.

Beverly was chartered in 1790 and is one of the oldest towns in the state. It was named for Beverly Randolph, mother of Edmund Randolph, Governor of Virginia from 1786 to 1788. The town was formerly known as Edmundton and it was the county seat until Elkins was granted that distinction in 1900.

Randolph County Notables

James E. Allen (1911-1971). US Commissioner of Education under Richard Nixon.

Dr. Joseph G. Allen (1913-1992). James Allen's brother, international expert on blood plasma.

William Wallace Barron (1911-1985). Governor of West Virginia, 1961-1965.

Henry Gassaway Davis (1823-1916). Financier and United States Senator, 1871-1883.

Stephen Benton Elkins (1841-1911). United States Senator, 1895-1911, and Secretary of War 1891-1893. Early developer of the city of Elkins. His wife, Hallie Davis Elkins, was the daughter of Senator Henry Gassaway Davis and the mother of Senator Davis Elkins and may be the only woman so related to three US senators.

Albert H. "Big Sleepy" Glenn (1904-1965). At Elkins High School, set national scholastic football scoring record in 1922 (351 points and 49 touchdowns). A great player at WVU.

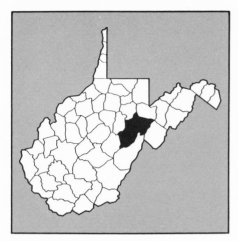

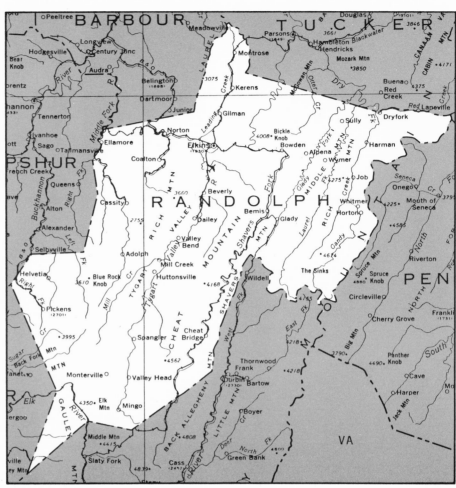

ECONOMIC PROFILE

Poverty status (all persons)	21.9%
65 and older	17.9%
Farms/value of farm products sold	383/$5.33 million
Retail sales	$138.89 million
Home ownership	74.5%
Value added by mining	$33.9 million
Median home value	$46,000
Median rent	$202/mo.

Dr. Marshall "Little Sleepy" Glenn (1908-1980). Also outstanding football and basketball player at Elkins High School and WVU.

Marshall "Biggie" Goldberg (1917-). All-state in football and basketball at Elkins High School, All-American at the University of Pittsburgh, all-pro in NFL.

Ray Harm (1927-). US Army veteran, one of the world's leading wildlife artists.

Mary Kinnan (1763-1848). Survived a captivity with the Delaware Indians, 1791-1794.

Herman G. Kump (1877-1962). Governor of West Virginia, 1933-1937.

Jennings Randolph (1902-). Congressman and United States Senator, 1958-1984.

Howard Sutherland (1865-1950). United States Senator, 1917-1923.

RANDOLPH COUNTY

Land in square miles	1,040
Total population	27,803
Percentage rural	73.3
Percentage female population	50.6
Percentage African-American population	0.8
Median age	35.4
Birth rate per 1,000 pop.	12.4
Percentage 65 and older	15.8
Median family income	$21,522

Educational attainment

Percent high school graduate or higher	65.9
Percent bachelor's degree or higher	11.9

Randolph

Bibliography

Bosworth, Albert S. *A History of Randolph County, West Virginia, From Its Earliest Exploration and Settlement to the Present Time.* [Elkins?] 1916. Reprinted: Parsons, McClain Printing Co., 1975.

Kek, Anna Dale. *Randolph County Profile—1976: A Handbook of the County.* Parsons, McClain Printing Co., 1976.

Maxwell, Hu. *The History of Randolph County, West Virginia.* Morgantown, The Acme Publishing Co., 1898. Reprinted: Parsons, McClain Printing Co., 1961.

Ritchie County

Ritchie County is located in the west-central part of the state. The county is hilly and much of it is forested. The area was explored in the 1770's but remained sparsely settled for decades. Ritchie County was formed in 1843 from parts of Harrison, Lewis, and Wood counties. The county was named for Thomas Ritchie (1778-1854), a Virginia journalist and politician. The county developed rapidly with the construction of two turnpikes and the Parkersburg branch of the Baltimore and Ohio Railroad through the area. In 1850, the county had a population of 3,902, which grew to 6,817 ten years later.

The economy of Ritchie County was long based on small farming. However, oil and gas production became important during the 1890's and early 1900's, and the economy expanded rapidly. Population reached 18,901 in 1900, the highest in the county's history. The boom was short-lived, and population declined steadily to 10,145 in 1970. However, an improved economy has given rise to an increase in population in recent years.

Harrisville, with a population in 1990 of 1,838, is the county seat. The town was laid out by Thomas Harris in 1832. The town's first name was Solus, then changed to Harrisville, after its founder, in 1843. Later, it was renamed Ritchie Court House, because a town had already been named Harrisville in Virginia. In 1892, the town was renamed Harrisville, this time in honor of the founding Harris' nephew, General Thomas Harris.

Mountain was renamed from Mole Hill, thanks to the efforts of Mrs. Florence Haymond in the 1940's. It was the home of John J. Cornwell, governor of the state 1916-1920.

Pennsboro, with a population of 1,282 in 1990, is the oldest town in the county. The town hosts the annual Ritchie County Fair, one of the largest fairs in the state and the first to be established.

Ritchie County Notables

John J. Cornwell (1867-1953). Governor of West Virginia, 1917-1921.

Thomas M. Harris (1813-1906). Physician and general in the Union Army during the Civil War.

A. Karl Summers (1904-1985). Built up a photo-finishing business in Parkersburg into one of America's largest.

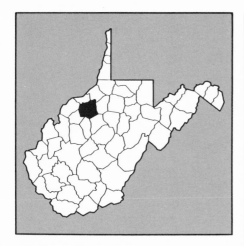

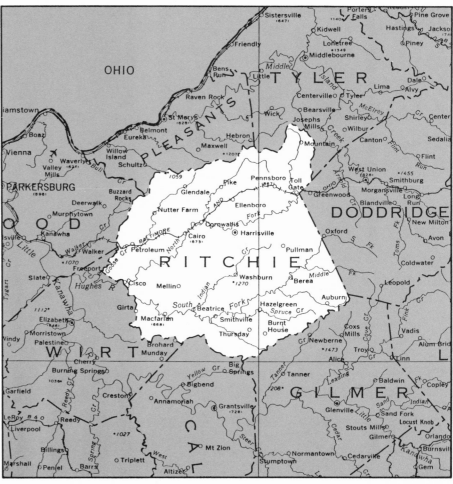

ECONOMIC PROFILE

Poverty status (all persons)	26.0%
65 and older	22.1%
Farms/value of farm products sold	325/$2.37 million
Retail sales	$36.05 million
Home ownership	80.0%
Value added by mining	NA
Median home value	$32,400
Median rent	$147/mo.

Bibliography

Lowther, Minnie Kendall. *History of Ritchie County.* Wheeling, Wheeling News Litho. Co., 1911. Reprinted: [n.p., Eloise B. Summers, 1967.]

Ritchie County Historical Society. *The History of Ritchie County, West Virginia to 1980.* [Harrisville], 1980.

RITCHIE COUNTY

Land in square miles	454
Total population	10,233
Percentage rural	100
Percentage female population	51.4
Percentage African-American population	0.1
Median age	36.4
Birth rate per 1,000 pop.	12.3
Percentage 65 and older	17.3
Median family income	$20,584

Educational attainment

Percent high school graduate or higher	61.5
Percent bachelor's degree or higher	6.0

Roane County

Spencer (population 2,799) is the home of the Black Walnut Festival every October and the modern Roane County Courthouse. (L. Victor Haines, WVU Photographic Services)

Roane County is one of the west-central counties of the state, and lies midway between the Little Kanawha and Kanawha rivers. The region was first visited by a non-Indian in 1772 when Jesse Hughes, a scout for the English army during Lord Dunmore's War, explored the Little Kanawha River basin. However, there was no significant settlement until well after the turn of the century. Roane County was formed in 1856 from parts of Kanawha, Jackson, and Gilmer counties. The new county was named for Judge Spencer Roane (1762-1822), a distinguished member of the Supreme Court of Appeals of Virginia. At the time, the county had a population of about 5,000.

Roane County remained poor and sparsely settled until the 1870's. Then the development of oil and gas fields brought both people and prosperity. Population more than doubled between 1870 and 1900 and peaked at over 21,000 in 1910. The depletion of the oil and gas fields resulted in a decline in population and economic activity during the following decades. However, improved transportation and the growth of light industry have in recent years brought renewed prosperity to the area.

Spencer, the county seat, was settled as early as 1812. The town was known first as Tanners Crossroads and then as New California. The name was changed to Spencer (after Spencer Roane) in 1858. The town had a population of 737 in 1900 which grew to 2,799 by 1980, but dropped to 2,279 in 1990. It is the location of Spencer Hospital, a state mental institution first opened in 1893.

Roane County Notables

William M. "Mil" Batten (1909-). Prominent businessman who became CEO of J.C. Penney, Inc., and Chairman of the New York Stock Exchange.

Harry Chapman Woodyard (1867-1929). One of the few people to serve three separate terms in the US Congress, 1902-1911, 1916-1923, and 1925-1927.

Bibliography

Bishop, William Henry. *History of Roane County, West Virginia from the Time of its Exploration to A.D. 1927.* Spencer, W. H. Bishop, 1927.

"Hardesty's Roane County." *West Virginia Heritage Encyclopedia.* Supplemental Series, vol. 5.

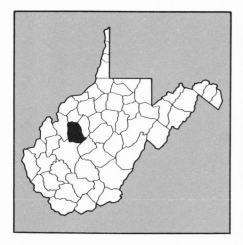

ECONOMIC PROFILE

Poverty status (all persons)	28.1%
65 and older	26.6%
Farms/value of farm products sold	460/$2.05 million
Retail sales	$56.55 million
Home ownership	78.0%
Value added by mining	NA
Median home value	$36,600
Median rent	$173/mo.

ROANE COUNTY

Land in square miles	484
Total population	15,120
Percentage rural	100
Percentage female population	50.8
Percentage African-American population	0.0
Median age	36.0
Birth rate per 1,000 pop.	12.1
Percentage 65 and older	15.5
Median family income	$17,898

Educational attainment

Percent high school graduate or higher	57.2
Percent bachelor's degree or higher	6.6

Summers County

John Henry Memorial above the Big Bend Tunnel that the folk song made famous. (L. Victor Haines, WVU Photographic Services)

Summers County is located in the southeastern part of the state. The terrain is mountainous and rough. Three major rivers flow through parts of the county—the Greenbrier, the Bluestone, and the New. The area began to be settled as early as the 1770's, but the population was sparse and scattered for many decades. The area was too rough and remote to be very attractive to settlers, and the few who ventured in depended for their livelihood on self-sufficient family farms.

Summers County was created in 1871 from parts of Greenbrier, Fayette, Mercer, and Monroe counties. The county was named after George W. Summers (1807-1868), a noted jurist and legislator. By 1880, the county had a population of 9,033.

The construction of the Chesapeake and Ohio Railroad that began in 1868 was the single most important development in the history of the county. People came in large numbers to build and maintain the railroad. The growing population required stores, banks, schools, and other services which gave employment to still others. Population exceeded 18,000 by 1910 and peaked at 20,468 in 1930, when it started to decline to 13,213 in 1970. The past decades have seen an increase in population, caused in large part by the growth of the recreational and tourist industries. Such facilities as those offered by Pipestem State Park have attracted increasing numbers of tourists.

Summers County has a secure place in the history of American folklore. The story has it that in 1872, during the construction of the Big Bend Tunnel, John Henry had his famous contest with the steam drill. The legend of John Henry is known in numerous versions throughout the country.

Hinton, the county seat, is located at the confluence of the Greenbrier and New rivers. It was founded in 1831 by John Hinton. The town grew slowly until the Chesapeake & Ohio Railroad arrived in the early 1870's. In 1990, the city had a population of 3,433.

Summers County Notables

John Edward Faulconer (1903-1981). Long-time editor, publisher, and owner of Hinton newspapers, and motivator behind Pipestem State Park.

William Hinton (1833-1905). Inventor of the trigonometer and other engineering devices.

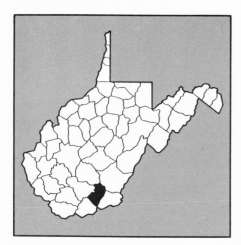

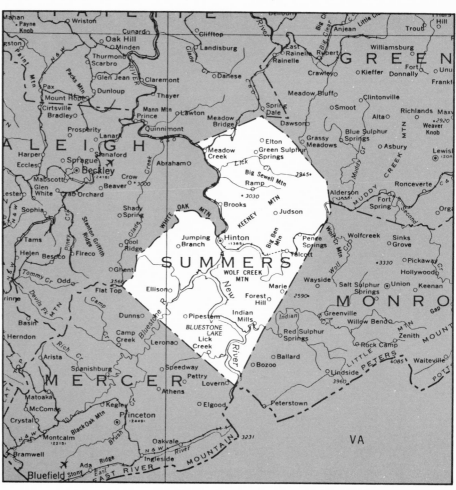

ECONOMIC PROFILE

Poverty status (all persons)	24.5%
65 and older	21.2%
Farms/value of farm products sold	317/$2.53 million
Retail sales	$35.22 million
Home ownership	76.7%
Value added by mining	NA
Median home value	$34,800
Median rent	$166/mo.

Thomas Jefferson Lilly (1878-1956). Congressman and W.Va. Commissioner of Accounts.

Dale Ratliff (1930 -). Hinton native who became president and CEO of Max Factor and Company, one of the largest cosmetic companies in the world. Married the former Betty Messer, also of Hinton.

Bibliography

Chappell, Louis *W. John Henry: A FolkLore Study.* Jena, Frommannsche Verlag, Walter Biederman, 1933. Reprinted: Port Washington, N.Y., Kennikat Press, 1968.

Lively, Lester. *Historical Summers County* (n.p., 1963).

Miller, James Henry. *History of Summers County from the Earliest Settlement to the Present Time.* Hinton, 1908.

SUMMERS COUNTY

Land in square miles	353
Total population	14,204
Percentage rural	75.8
Percentage female population	55.0
Percentage African-American population	5.1
Median age	37.3
Birth rate per 1,000 pop.	8.6
Percentage 65 and older	17.5
Median family income	$20,076

Educational attainment

Percent high school graduate or higher	58.0
Percent bachelor's degree or higher	8.5

Taylor County

Mother's Day Church in Grafton, about 1911. Anna Jarvis, whose birthplace is in nearby Webster, started Mother's Day on May 10, 1908. (West Virginia and Regional History Collection, WVU Libraries)

Taylor County is located in the north-central part of West Virginia on the Appalachian plateau. The terrain is hilly, though there is flat and rolling land for agriculture and industry along the major water courses. The land is drained by the Tygart River and its tributaries. The first white man known to have entered the area was probably John Simpson, a trapper for the Hudson Bay Company, who crossed the Tygart River on his way westward in 1768. Shortly thereafter, Thomas Merrifield and Captain John Booth made settlements along present-day Booth's Creek.

The area comprising present-day Taylor County remained sparsely settled until the opening decades of the 19th century. However, by 1844 it was sufficiently populated to warrant the formation of a new county, and in that year Taylor County was formed from parts of Harrison, Barbour, and Marion counties. It was named for John Taylor (1753-1824) of Caroline County, Virginia, an author and statesman. In 1850, the county had a population of 5,367. The area of the county was enlarged in 1856 by the addition of a small portion of Marion County.

In 1853, the Baltimore and Ohio Railroad was completed to Wheeling. The railroad passed through Taylor County at a point just south of Fetterman. The development of the railroad facilities at this point brought about the birth of the town of Grafton. In 1857, the Northwestern Virginia Railroad, later taken over by the B & O, was completed from Grafton to Parkersburg. Located at the junction of these two major lines, Grafton became an important transportation center.

The economy of Taylor County was for many years based almost entirely on agriculture, and it remains an important element today. However, the development of Grafton as a major rail center provided considerable employment, as did the growth of the coal industry. Coal production began in the late 1880's and increased to over one million tons in 1920. Production declined steadily thereafter, and coal is now of only minor importance to the area's economy. Taylor County's population peaked at 19,919 in 1940 and declined to 13,878 thirty years later. However, the 1990 census showed an increase in population.

Grafton, the county seat, was chartered in 1856 and named for John Grafton, a civil engineer employed by the B & O Railroad. The town was

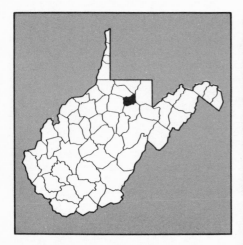

ECONOMIC PROFILE

Poverty status (all persons)	22.9%
65 and older	18.7%
Farms/value of farm products sold	245/$3.13 million
Retail sales	$42.98 million
Home ownership	76.2%
Value added by mining	NA
Median home value	$34,200
Median rent	$159/mo.

made the county seat in 1878. The only National Cemetery in the state is located here, as is the Mother's Day Shrine. In 1990, the city had a population of 5,524.

Taylor County Notables

Clair Bee (1900-1982). Hall of Fame basketball coach, one of the greatest of all time, primarily at Long Island University and the NBA Baltimore Bullets.

C. E. "Jim" Compton (1915-). Coal and health systems entrepreneur whose Grafton Coal Company closed in 1994 after 52 years.

Floyd Scotty Hamilton (1921-1976). All-state basketball star at Grafton High School, All-American at WVU.

TAYLOR COUNTY

Land in square miles	174
Total population	15,144
Percentage rural	63.5
Percentage female population	51.6
Percentage African-American population	0.6
Median age	35.7
Birth rate per 1,000 pop.	12.2
Percentage 65 and older	16.2
Median family income	$22,357

Educational attainment

Percent high school graduate or higher	66.0
Percent bachelor's degree or higher	8.1

Anna Jarvis (1864-1948). Founder of Mother's Day in honor of her mother, Anna Reeves Jarvis (1832-1902).

John Barton Payne (1855-1935). US Secretary of the Interior, 1920-1921.

Francis Benjamin Johnston (1864-1952). Born in Grafton, she was an early reporter and superior photographer.

George Preston Marshall (1896-1968). Innovative businessman, owner of the Washington Redskins of the National Football League.

John T. McGraw (1850-1920). Industrialist and politician, national figure in the Democratic Party, twice candidate for US Senator.

Bibliography

Grafton Centennial Committee. *Grafton's Centennial,* 1856-1956. Grafton, 1956.

Shingleton, George A. *Grafton and Taylor County During the Civil War Days and Points of Interest*. Taylor County Historical Society, 1961.

Tucker County

Above: Skiing at Canaan Valley. (Tom Evans, West Virginia Department of Commerce)

Right: Blackwater Falls State Park (L. Victor Haines, WVU Photographic Services)

Tucker County lies in the northeastern part of the state and includes some of its most rugged and mountainous terrain. It is drained almost entirely by the Cheat River. The first permanent settlers in the area were the Parsons brothers, Thomas and John, who came from the South Branch of the Potomac and settled about 1772 at Holly Meadows on the Cheat River. In 1774, John Minear, a German immigrant, founded a settlement where the town of St. George now stands. Tucker County was formed in 1856 from the northern portion of Randolph County, by an act of the Virginia General Assembly. It was named for Henry St. George Tucker (1780-1848), an eminent jurist and statesman of Virginia. In 1860, the county had a population of 1,428.

Tucker County has always been primarily an agricultural area, but the large reserves of coal, limestone, shale, and timber have encouraged industrial development. With the coming of the railroads in the last years of the 19th century, the county began an era of rapid economic expansion. In 1889, the West Virginia Central and Pittsburgh Railway Company completed a line from Elkins northward through Parsons and Thomas to Piedmont in Mineral County, linking Tucker County with the Baltimore and Ohio main line. This railway made possible the development of the timber and coal resources, and by 1911 the coal mines of the county were producing 2,213,947 tons—an all-time high. By 1910, the population of the area had grown to 18,675 and the county boasted two railroads, two paper mills, three tanneries, fifteen large sawmills, ten logging railways, lime kilns, stone crushers, and almost a thousand coke ovens.

The population of Tucker County declined substantially after 1910 to 7,447 in 1970, but has since rebounded. Besides agricultural products, the county produces leather, textiles, and charcoal. The coal industry continues to operate, though on a much smaller scale, with 332,000 tons produced in 1983, all by surface mines. The recreation and tourist industries have become increasingly important. Canaan Valley State Park and Blackwater Falls State Park and a part of the Monongahela National Forest are located in Tucker County.

Parsons, the county seat, is located on Shaver's Fork of the Cheat River. It was incorporated in 1893 and named for Ward Parsons, a pioneer who owned the land on which the town was built. Its population was 1,453 in 1980.

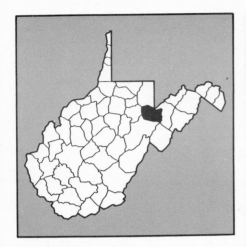

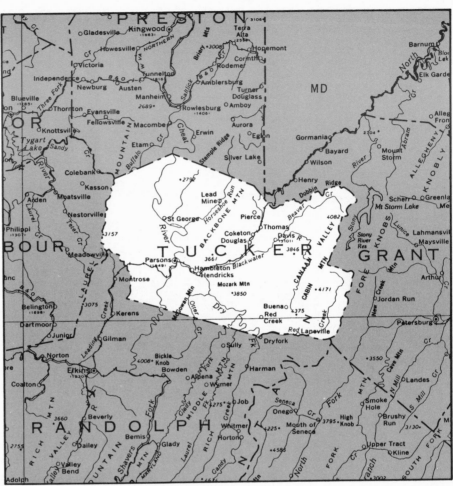

ECONOMIC PROFILE

Poverty status (all persons)	17.0%
65 and older	20.1%
Farms/value of farm products sold	160/$1.07 million
Retail sales	$23.33 million
Home ownership	80.4%
Value added by mining	NA
Median home value	$38,200
Median rent	$168/mo.

Tucker County Notables

John J. Knight (1899-1988). Long-time coach and athletic director at Bethany College, 1930-1969; President of the NAIA, 1959-1960.

Hu Maxwell (1850-1927). Author and historian.

George Smith (1924-). Director of West Virginia's largest publisher, McClain Printing Company of Parsons.

Bibliography

Fansler, Homer Floyd. *History of Tucker County, West Virginia.* Parsons, McClain Printing Co., 1962.

Maxwell, Hu. *History of Tucker County, West Virginia, From the Earliest Exploration and Settlements to the Present Time.* Kingwood, Preston Publishing Co., 1884. Reprinted: Parsons, McClain Printing Co., 1971.

Mott, Pearle G. *History of Davis and Canaan Valley.* Parsons, McClain Printing Co., 1972.

TUCKER COUNTY

Land in square miles	421
Total population	7,728
Percentage rural	100
Percentage female population	51.4
Percentage African-American population	0.1
Median age	37.2
Birth rate per 1,000 pop.	12.0
Percentage 65 and older	16.7
Median family income	$22,825

Educational attainment

Percent high school graduate or higher	64.0
Percent bachelor's degree or higher	8.6

Tyler County

Victorian Wells Inn in Sistersville.

Tyler County is located in the northwest section of the state, with the Ohio River forming its western boundary. Except for the river valley, the county's terrain is very hilly and broken. The region was not permanently settled until after the American Revolution. The first settlers seem to have been Thomas and John Williamson in 1792. They were soon followed by many others in the last decade of the 18th century. Tyler County was created from Ohio County in 1814, and named in honor of John Tyler (1747-1813), a governor of Virginia. Six years later, when the county's population was first counted, Tyler County had a population of 2,314.

The Tyler County High School in Middlebourne, constructed in 1906-1908, was the first county system high school in West Virginia, and made West Virginia only the eighth state to establish a county school system. Classes began on September 28, 1908; the school building is under consideration for the National Register of Historic Places.

Tyler County's economy depended almost entirely on agriculture until the 1890's. Then a great oil and gas boom developed, which lasted for a little over a decade. In 1894, the famous "Big Moses" well was drilled and produced 100 million cubic feet of gas per day. Money and people poured in, and by 1900 the county's population reached an all-time high of 18,252. However, the population began to drop with the decline of oil and gas production and reached a low of 9,796 in 1990.

Middlebourne, the county seat, was established in 1813. Its name is said to come from the fact that the site was approximately halfway between the Pennsylvania state line and the salt well on the Kanawha River. In 1990, the town had a population of 922.

Sistersville, named in honor of the sisters Sarah and Delilah Wells, is the county's largest town, with a population in 1990 of 1,797. Established in 1815, Sistersville, on the Ohio River, was the center of the oil and gas in-dustry. The town's many fine homes testify to the wealth generated by the industry during the boom times.

Tyler County Notables

Robert Edward Lee Allen (1865-1951). Educator and Congressman.

A. Wilbur Cooper (1892-1973). Hall of Fame baseball pitcher who won 216 games while losing 178; his 202 wins for the Pirates are the most for a Pittsburgh pitcher.

Edward I. Hanlon (1887-1963). Multimillionaire oil man and banker.

Cecil H. Underwood (1922-   ). Governor of West Virginia, 1957-1961. Governor elect, 1996.

Bibliography

"Hardesty's Tyler County." *West Virginia Heritage Encyclopedia.* Supplemental Series, vol. 1.

Kimball, Charles N. "Sistersville." *West Virginia Review,* June 1936, pp. 282-284.

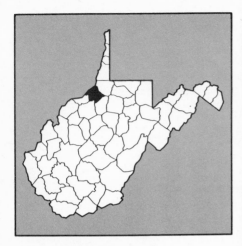

ECONOMIC PROFILE

Poverty status (all persons)	18.3%
65 and older	20.7%
Farms/value of farm products sold	260/$1.57 million
Retail sales	$22.53 million
Home ownership	82.0%
Value added by mining	NA
Median home value	$43,200
Median rent	$171/mo.

TYLER COUNTY

Land in square miles	258
Total population	9,796
Percentage rural	90.7
Percentage female population	50.9
Percentage African-American population	0.0
Median age	36.3
Birth rate per 1,000 pop.	12.1
Percentage 65 and older	15.4
Median family income	$25,462

Educational attainment

Percent high school graduate or higher	68.7
Percent bachelor's degree or higher	9.0

Upshur County

Benedum Campus Community Center at West Virginia Wesleyan College in Buckhannon. (West Virginia Wesleyan College)

Upshur County is located in the central part of the state, in an area often referred to as the Allegheny Highlands. The terrain of the county is hilly to mountainous. Most of the county is drained by the Buckhannon River, which flows through the central part of the county. The Little Kanawha River drains a small section of the southwestern section of the county, while the Middle Fork River drains the eastern part and forms the boundary with Randolph County.

John and Samuel Pringle, deserters from the English army at Fort Pitt, came to the Buckhannon River Valley in 1764 and lived for a time in a huge, hollow sycamore tree near the mouth of Turkey Run. The Pringles were soon followed by other settlers from the Shenandoah and Potomac river valleys. The number of settlements increased dramatically after the Treaty of Greenville in 1795 made all of west-ern Virginia secure from Indian attack. Upshur County was created in 1851 from parts of Lewis, Barbour, and Randolph counties, and named for Abel Parker Upshur (1780-1844), a Virginia jurist and Secretary of State under President Tyler. In 1860, the county had a population of 7,292.

The virgin forests of the county were commercially exploited after the completion of a railroad from Weston to Buckhannon in 1883. Later, in 1891, the line was extended, linking the entire county with the Baltimore and Ohio Railroad mainline at Fairmont. Coal production began in 1906, when 6,506 tons were mined. By 1925, production had increased to 1,066,422 tons, but it began to decline soon after World War II and by 1970 it had dropped to 879,319 tons. However, production has increased in recent years. Despite slight dips in population in 1960 and 1970, the population of the county has steadily increased since its creation in 1851. In 1920, the county had a population of 17,851. In 1970 it was 19,092. In 1990 the population was almost 23,000.

This county made national news in November 1982 when Mrs. Rosalie Henry was elected to the county Board of Education, thus creating the first all-woman school board in the nation, according to Director Phil Smith of the National School Boards Association. The other women on the Upshur board were Miss Kay Starkey, Mrs. Colleen Folger, Mrs. Jennie Pyles, and Mrs. Linda Woodburn Hoover.

Buckhannon, the county seat, was established in 1816 and was incorporated in 1833. The town was named by the first white settlers for Buck-on-go-ho-nan, a chief of the Delaware Indians. It is the home of West Virginia Wesleyan College. Established in 1890 as the West Virginia Conference Seminary by the Methodist Episcopal Church, West Virginia Wesleyan today has an enrollment of approximately 1,700.

Upshur County Notables

Alonzo Beecher Brooks (1873-1944). Author and naturalist.

Stephen Coonts (1944-). Buckhannon native and WVU alumnus who is a 1980s/1990s best-selling novelist *(Flight of the Intruder, Cannibal Queen, etc.)*

Daniel D. T. Farnsworth (1819-1892). Governor of West Virginia, 1869.

Charles Harper (1922-). World War II Army veteran and distinguished nature artist.

Pare Lorentz (1915- 1992). Father of the documentary film.

A. F. "Nate" Rohrbaugh (1902-1997). Outstanding in football and basketball at Buckhannon High School and WVU. Great coach at Glenville State.

C. B. "Cebe" Ross (1902-1953). All-state quarterback at Buckhannon High School, coach at West Virginia Wesleyan and Morris Harvey, now University of Charleston.

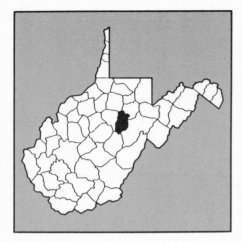

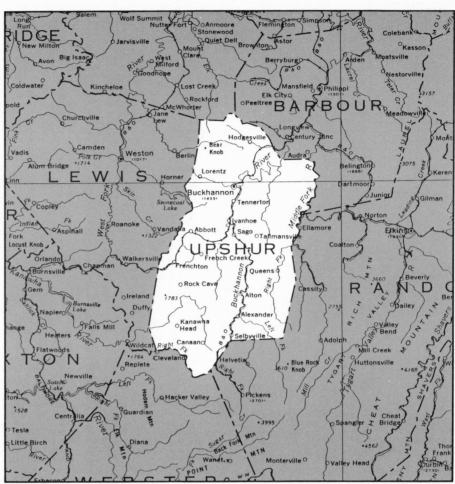

ECONOMIC PROFILE

Poverty status (all persons)	21.2%
65 and older	17.1%
Farms/value of farm products sold	354/$2.38 million
Retail sales	$103.69 million
Home ownership	75.5%
Value added by mining	NA
Median home value	$47,900
Median rent	$200/mo.

D. K. "Coach" Shroyer (1898-1974). Three-sport star at Buckhannon-Upshur High School and West Virginia Wesleyan. Long-time coach, president of Beckley College, 1960-1968.

Bibliography

Cutright, William B. *The History of Upshur County, West Virginia From Its Earliest Exploration and Settlement to the Present Time.* (Buckhannon) 1907. Reprinted, with Family History Index, compiled by Hilda L. Sayre: Buckhannon, Upshur County Historical Society, 1977.

Hornbeck, Betty. *Upshur Brothers of The Blue and The Gray.* Parsons, McClain Printing Co., 1967.

Morgan, French. *Yesterdays of Buckhannon and Upshur.* Buckhannon, The Republican-Delta, 1963.

UPSHUR COUNTY

Land in square miles	355
Total population	22,867
Percentage rural	74.2
Percentage female population	51.1
Percentage African-American population	0.5
Median age	33.4
Birth rate per 1,000 pop.	14.1
Percentage 65 and older	14.7
Median family income	$22,267

Educational attainment

Percent high school graduate or higher	64.3
Percent bachelor's degree or higher	12.0

Wayne County

Beech Fork State Park features this 760-acre lake. (Edwin D. Michael)

Wayne County is located in the extreme southwestern part of the state. It lies along the lower course of the Big Sandy River and for some distance along the Ohio River. Permanent settlement began about 1795. The availability of river transportation made the area easy to reach and attracted many settlers.

Wayne County was formed in 1842 from part of Cabell County and named in honor of General Anthony Wayne, hero of the Revolution and the Battle of Fallen Timbers. By the census of 1850, Wayne County had a population of 4,760. Except for some relatively minor skirmishes, Wayne County escaped the ravages of the Civil War. The county began to grow rapidly after the war, and the population tripled (to 23,619) between 1870 and 1900.

A small coal industry began to develop about 1910, and there has long been some production of oil and gas. Agriculture has continued to play a significant role. However, Wayne County's prosperity and relatively steady increase in population may be attributed in large part to its proximity to the Huntington area. There an increasing number of Wayne County residents find employment, while many with jobs in the metropolitan area have built homes in less congested Wayne County. The county experienced a very sharp increase in population (22.5 percent) between 1970 and 1980, and in 1990 had over 41,000 people.

Wayne, the county seat, was selected as the seat upon the organization of the county in 1842. It was first known as Trout's Hill, after Abraham Trout on whose land the town was established. The name was changed to Fairview in 1882 and to Wayne in 1911. In 1990, Wayne had a population of 1,128.

Wayne County Notables

Admiral Harry F. Bruns (1889-1947). Graduate of Ceredo High School, United States Naval Academy, and Rensselaer Polytechnic Institute. Admiral Bruns served in the Navy through World Wars I and II, and as Director of the Bureau of Yards and Docks—both Atlantic and Pacific coasts—until his death.

Fannie Belle Fleming ("Blaze Starr") (1923-). Nightclub stripper, paramour of Louisiana Governor Russell Long.

Bibliography

Taylor, Mildred. *History of Wayne County, West Virginia.* Wayne, 1963.

Thomson, C. W. *History of Ceredo and Kenova.* (Ceredo 1995-).

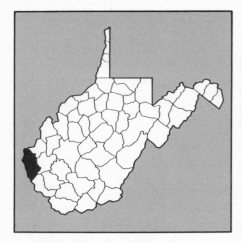

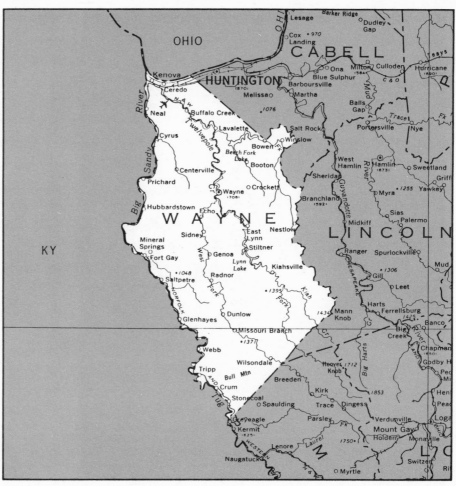

ECONOMIC PROFILE

Poverty status	
(all persons)	21.8%
65 and older	20.6%
Farms/value of farm products sold	193/$886,000
Retail sales	$96.74 million
Home ownership	76.6%
Value added by mining	NA
Median home value	$46,700
Median rent	$213/mo.

WAYNE COUNTY

Land in square miles	508
Total population	41,636
Percentage rural	71.1
Percentage female population	51.7
Percentage African-American population	0.0
Median age	35.3
Birth rate per 1,000 pop.	12.1
Percentage 65 and older	13.7
Median family income	$23,525

Educational attainment

Percent high school graduate or higher	63.1
Percent bachelor's degree or higher	9.0

Webster County

Left Fork of Holly River. (Gerald S. Ratliff, West Virginia Department of Commerce)

Webster County is located in the central part of the state. The county is mostly mountainous, with altitudes ranging from 1,000 to over 3,800 feet. The county is drained by seven rivers: the Elk, Gauley, Williams, Birch, Holly, Cranberry, and Little Kanawha, all of which flow in a general westerly direction. Adam Stroud was probably the first white settler in the area now known as Webster County. He made a settlement on a tributary of the Gauley River now called Stroud's Creek in about 1769. Few settlers followed Stroud, for the area was too rugged and remote to be attractive.

In 1860, the Virginia Assembly created Webster County from parts of Nicholas, Braxton, and Randolph counties. It was named in honor of Daniel Webster, and was the last county created before the separation of West Virginia from Virginia. The war interrupted the organization of the county, and during this period, the governmental functions of neither Virginia nor West Virginia prevailed. No taxes were collected nor courts held. According to legend, this void of authority was filled by the "Independent State of Webster," supposedly a fully organized state government with George M. Sawyers as Governor. At the close of the war, the actual organization of the county continued, and in 1865 county and district officers were elected. The 1860 census showed a population of 1,555 living in the county.

The earliest occupations of the settlers in Webster County were farming and lumbering. The first lumbering operations were located along the Elk River and its major tributaries. Trees were cut and floated down the Elk to a mill in Charleston. In 1899, the first railroad was built in the county, the West Virginia and Pittsburgh. Other branch lines were soon built and the timber industry grew rapidly. The prosperity brought about by the railroads and the exploitation of the county's timber resources were responsible for a doubling of the county's population from 4,783 to 9,682 in the period from 1890 to 1910.

Commercial coal production began in Webster County about 1917, but did not reach the 100,000-ton level until 1929. Production peaked at just short of two million tons in 1945 and then began to decline; it was 877,588 tons in 1983. The population of Webster County continued to increase until 1940, when it peaked at 18,080. It declined until 1970, when it numbered 9,809, but has increased in recent years. Holly River State Park and part of the Monongahela National Forest are located in Webster County.

Webster Springs, the county seat, is located on the Elk River at Back Fork. The town was first called Fork Lick but was incorporated in 1892 as Addison, after Addison McLaughlin, on whose land the town was laid out. The population of the town was 297 in 1900 and is approximately 1,000 at the present time. While the official name of the town remains Addison, it is generally referred to as Webster Springs, the post office designation.

Webster County Notables

Arden Cogar (1935-   ). National champion woodchopper.

Eli C. "Rimfire" Hamrick (1868-1945). Noted hunter chosen as the "typical Mountaineer" for the bronze statue at the capitol in Charleston.

Hobert (1909-1969) and Hubert (1909-1946) Skidmore. Twin brothers and award-winning authors.

Bibliography
Chapman, Berlin B. *Education in Central West Virginia, 1910-1975.* Morgantown, West Virginia University Foundation, 1974.

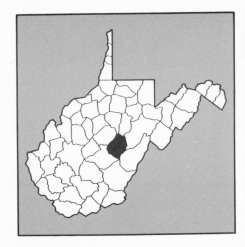

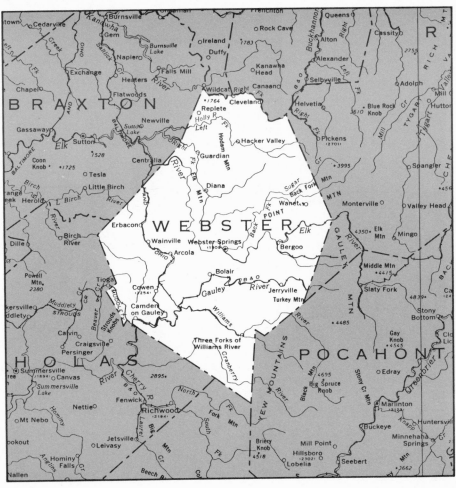

ECONOMIC PROFILE

Poverty status (all persons)	34.8%
65 and older	22.3%
Farms/value of farm products sold	105/$191,000
Retail sales	$27.19 million
Home ownership	78.4%
Value added by mining	$22.4 million
Median home value	$29,700
Median rent	$144/mo.

Dodrill, William C. *Moccasin Tracks, and Other Imprints.* Charleston, Lovett Printing Co., 1915. Reprinted: Parsons, McClain Printing Co., 1974. Miller, Sampson Newton. Annals of Webster County, West Virginia, Before and Since Organization, 1860. Webster Springs, Sampson N. Miller, 1969.

WEBSTER COUNTY

Land in square miles	556
Total population	10,729
Percentage rural	100
Percentage female population	51.5
Percentage African-American population	0.0
Median age	34.8
Birth rate per 1,000 pop.	12.8
Percentage 65 and older	15.5
Median family income	$15,489

Educational attainment

Percent high school graduate or higher	46.5
Percent bachelor's degree or higher	5.6

Wetzel County

Coal barges on the Ohio River. (L. Victor Haines, WVU Photographic Services)

Wetzel County is located in the northwest part of the state beside the Ohio River and forms the base of West Virginia's Northern Panhandle. Its terrain is rough and uneven except for the river valley. A number of adventurers and explorers went through the area from the 1750's to the 1770's. One of the first men to make his home in Wetzel County was Edward Dulin who, in 1773, settled near present-day New Martinsville. Others soon followed him in establishing homes beside the Ohio River. Wetzel County was formed in 1846 from Tyler County. The county was named for Lewis Wetzel, a famous frontiersman and Indian fighter. At the time of its formation the county had a population of about 4,200.

Wetzel County, though linked to the outside world by the Ohio River and the Baltimore and Ohio Railroad, remained largely agricultural until the late 1880's when oil and gas were discovered. Within a few years, oil and gas wells were being drilled throughout most of the county. During the boom period from 1890 to 1900 the population jumped from 16,841 to 22,855. As the oil reserves were depleted, the county turned to industries such as glass and chemicals.

New Martinsville, the county seat, was chartered in 1838 by the General Assembly of Virginia. The town had a population of 228 by 1850 but did not reach 1,000 until 1900. At first the town was named Martinsville, but it was discovered that another town in Virginia had already been named Martinsville and the name was changed to New Martinsville. The town remains the center of county life and has a population of 6,705.

Wetzel County Notables

Doug Huff (1941-   ). Wheeling sports editor and author, a leading national scholastic sports authority.

Harley Martin Kilgore (1893-1956). US Senator from West Virginia, 1941-1956.

Mont McIntyre (1884-1953). Magnolia High School and WVU football star who coached at West Virginia Wesleyan and WVU.

Joseph C. Trees (1869-1943). Oil wildcatter who became a multimillionaire in partnership with Michael Benedum and John Kirkland.

Bibliography

McEldowney, John C., Jr. *History of Wetzel County, West Virginia.* (n.p.) 1901. Reprinted: (New Martinsville) Wetzel County Genealogical Society, 1980.

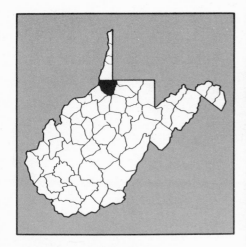

ECONOMIC PROFILE

Poverty status	
(all persons)	20.5%
65 and older	23.4%
Farms/value of farm products sold	203/$564,000
Retail sales	$111.91 million
Home ownership	77.3%
Value added by mining	NA
Median home value	$50,200
Median rent	$183/mo.

WETZEL COUNTY

Land in square miles	359
Total population	19,258
Percentage rural	55.3
Percentage female population	52.0
Percentage African-American population	0.1
Median age	36.1
Birth rate per 1,000 pop.	14.3
Percentage 65 and older	14.8
Median family income	$28,122

Educational attainment

Percent high school graduate or higher	70.1
Percent bachelor's degree or higher	10.4

Wirt County

Above: Wirt County Courthouse in Elizabeth.
(James E. Harding)

Right: Rubie Log Church, built in 1835 of
hand-hewn logs, retains its original
appearance. It is near Burning Springs where
West Virginia's first major oil field was
developed in the 1860's. (Rodney S. Collins)

Wirt County was created from Jackson and Wood counties in 1848. It was named after William Wirt (1772-1834), Virginia lawyer, author and Attorney General of the United States. The area along the Little Kanawha River, which traverses Wirt County from southeast to northwest, was settled as early as the 1780's. The early settlers carved out small farms and were largely self-sufficient. The area remained isolated and sparsely settled until the development of the Burning Springs oil field began in 1860. People flocked to Burning Springs and a sizable town appeared almost overnight. The population of the town was estimated to be approximately 6,000 in 1861— substantially greater than the present population of the entire county. However, the oil field was an attractive military target, and on May 9, 1863, a Confederate force under the command of General William E. Jones burned the town, wells, and equipment.

Burning Springs never recovered from its destruction at the hands of General Jones and gradually faded away. Its population was less than 500 by 1880, and what was for a few years a major settlement is now an unincorporated rural community. The petroleum industry revived after the Civil War, and Wirt County shared to some degree in the general prosperity. Population increased from 4,804 in 1870 to 10,284 in 1900, the peak year. However, the production of petroleum began to decline sharply, and there was no other industry to replace it. Wirt County became once again an area of small farms, woodland, and scattered villages. Population declined steadily and reached a low of 4,154 in 1970. However, recent years have seen a modest increase in gas and oil production and a growing recognition of the potential of the many recreational opportunities which the area offers.

Elizabeth, the county seat, is situated on the Little Kanawha River. The town was named for Elizabeth Woodyard Beauchamp, wife of an early settler. Elizabeth had a population of 900 in 1990.

Wirt County Notables
Raymond F. Morgan (1908-1997). Longtime member of the West Virginia House of Delegates.

Charles B. Smith (1844-1899). Congressman, Union Civil War veteran.

Bibliography
"Hardesty's Wirt County." West Virginia Heritage Encyclopedia. Supplemental Series, vol. 6.

Reed, Louis. Warning in Appalachia: A Study of Wirt County, West Virginia. Morgantown, West Virginia University Library, 1967.

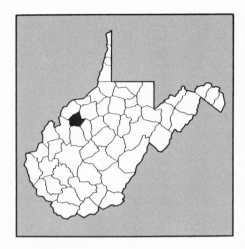

ECONOMIC PROFILE

Poverty status (all persons)	22.0%
65 and older	27.2%
Farms/value of farm products sold	221/$2.96 million
Retail sales	$6.29 million
Home ownership	81.3%
Value added by mining	NA
Median home value	$36,300
Median rent	$149/mo.

WIRT COUNTY

Land in square miles	235
Total population	5,192
Percentage rural	100
Percentage female population	51.0
Percentage African-American population	0.1
Median age	34.5
Birth rate per 1,000 pop.	11.0
Percentage 65 and older	14.3
Median family income	$21,193

Educational attainment

Percent high school graduate or higher	66.2
Percent bachelor's degree or higher	8.0

Wood County

Above: Slave labor built this house, named Oakland, from 1833 to 1843. Located at 1131 Seventh Street in Parkersburg. It was the home of James M. Stephenson. (Rodney S. Collins)

Other historic houses in Parkersburg—1034 Ann Street (right) and 1110 Ann Street (below). (James E. Harding)

Wood County is located in the northwest part of West Virginia along the Ohio River and is divided by the Little Kanawha River. The first European to explore this area appears to have been Celoron de Blainville. In the summer of 1749, he descended the Ohio River, planting lead plates along the river valley which proclaimed that the land belonged to France. The English settlers and traders paid no attention to his claims and moved into the area at will. Wood County was established in 1798 from the western part of Harrison County. The county was named in honor of James Wood, Governor of Virginia at the time of the county's creation. The 1800 census showed 1,217 persons living in the new county.

The most famous early resident was Harman Blennerhassett. In 1797, he built one of the most palatial homes west of the Alleghenies on what became Blennerhassett Island, just below Parkersburg in the Ohio Valley.

The splendor was short-lived, for Blennerhassett was ruined by the failure of the Burr-Blennerhassett conspiracy (1806), and his mansion was destroyed. The island is today a historical park. The outbreak of the Civil War found Wood County in favor of the Union. The leaders of Wood County were also the leaders of, first, the restored government of Virginia, and later, the movement to form a new state.

Wood County was an important trading area beginning in the 1790's. The completion of the Northwest Turnpike gave impetus to the county's growth. This economic expansion continued with the arrival of a branch line of the Baltimore and Ohio Railroad in 1857 and the development of the Burning Springs oil fields in the early 1860's. After the Civil War, Wood County prospered with the oil and gas trade. When oil and gas became less important, Wood County continued to grow by developing industry and commerce. The population grew from 11,046 in 1860 to 38,001 by 1910 and has continued to increase steadily (over 80,000 in 1990).

Parkersburg, the county seat, was named for Alexander Parker, who owned the land. The title to this land was contested by others, who had previously laid out the town of Newport. The matter went to court and in 1809, the courts ruled in favor of the Parker heirs. In 1810, the town's name officially became Parkersburg. The town grew slowly and had a

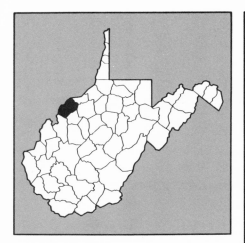

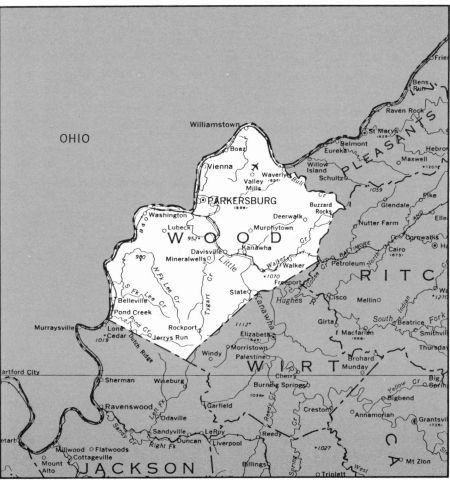

ECONOMIC PROFILE

Poverty status (all persons)	14.1%
65 and older	16.6%
Farms/value of farm products sold	520/$3.21 million
Retail sales	$641.97 million
Home ownership	73.8%
Value added by mining	NA
Median home value	$49,500
Median rent	$249/mo.

population of 2,493 in 1860. However, Parkersburg profited greatly from the oil and gas boom following the Civil War and became an important financial, industrial, and commercial center. Its population exceeded 8,000 by 1890 and more than doubled (to 17,842) in 1910. The present population is approximately 34,000. In 1971, the city became the home of Parkersburg Community College, the state's first community college, now part of West Virginia University with an enrollment of about 3,000.

Wood County Notables

Leonard Warner "Feets" Barnum (1913-). All-state in three sports at Parkersburg High School and football great at West Virginia Wesleyan.

Arthur I. Boreman (1823-1896). First Governor of West Virginia. He also served in the United States Senate 1869-1875.

WOOD COUNTY

Land in square miles	368
Total population	86,915
Percentage rural	34.1
Percentage female population	52.4
Percentage African-American population	0.9
Median age	36.0
Birth rate per 1,000 pop.	11.5
Percentage 65 and older	14.8
Median family income	$30,582

Educational attainment

Percent high school graduate or higher	73.2
Percent bachelor's degree or higher	13.5

Wood

Johnson N. Camden (1826-1908). Financier and United States Senator, 1881-1887, 1893-1895.

Richard C. Holblitzell (1888-1962). Major league first baseman for eleven years.

Jacob B. Jackson (1829-1893). Governor of West Virginia, 1881-1885.

Bernard McDonough (1905-1987). Multimillionaire industrialist and financier.

Earl "Greasy" Neale (1892-1973). Star football player (West Virginia Wesleyan) and coach (Washington and Jefferson College, WVU, NFL champion Philadelphia Eagles) took Washington and Jefferson College to the Rose Bowl in 1922. Also starred in baseball for the Cincinnati Reds.

Monroe Jackson Rathbone (1900-1976). Graduate of Parkersburg High School and Lehigh University, rose through the ranks to become Chairman and CEO of Standard Oil of New Jersey in the 1960s.

William E. Stevenson (1820-1883). Governor of West Virginia, 1869-1871.

Felix B. Stump (1894-1971). Admiral and commander of the U.S. Pacific forces, 1953-1958.

Marj Teague (1935-). Born in Williamstown, veteran of the US Marine Corps (1958-62), a prominent artist noted for commissioned portraits of John Glenn and Pearl Buck.

Albert B. White (1856-1941). Governor of West Virginia, 1901-1905.

Peter G. Van Winkle (1808-1872). United States Senator, 1863-1869.

Wyoming County

Golf course at Twin Falls State Park. (West Virginia Department of Natural Resources)

Wyoming County is located in the southern part of the state. Its terrain is generally rough and mountainous, drained by the Guyandotte River and its tributaries. The Mingo, Shawnee, and Wyandotte Indians used this region as a hunting ground. The first settlers were veterans of the Revolutionary War. Leading the way was John Cooke, who built his home near the present-day town of Oceana in 1799. Wyoming County was created in 1850 from Logan County. Why the county was named Wyoming is unclear. One source states that it was named for the Delaware Indian word meaning "large plains," but this does not describe the hilly countryside of the county. A more likely explanation is that the county was named for the Wyoming Indian tribe. The new county had a population of about 1,600.

Wyoming County remained isolated and sparsely populated until the turn of this century. Farming and lumbering were the only significant sources of income. The existence of the area's rich coal fields was well-known, but their exploitation had to await the arrival of the railroad. An adequate rail system began to be put in place about 1912, making possible a remarkable development of the coal industry. Coal production increased from approximately 40,000 tons in 1914 to 1,329,700 tons in 1920. By 1950, production was over six million tons; twenty years later it exceeded thirteen million tons. In 1983, some 8,253,000 tons of coal were produced in Wyoming County. The rapid growth of the coal industry caused a substantial increase in population. Population grew from 8,330 in 1900 to over 15,000 in 1920 and to 37,540 in 1950. However, reduction in coal mining has led to a drop in population (to about 29,000 in 1990).

Pineville, the county seat, is situated on the Guyandotte River. The first settlement near the site was made by Hiram Clay in 1863. The town was named after the pitch pine forest in the area. Pineville was incorporated in 1907. In that year the county seat was moved from Oceana to Pineville. In 1990, the town had a population of 865.

Wyoming County Notables

Krikor George Khorozian (1888-1952). Physician and medical researcher who made many discoveries, including the microkaryocyte cell.

William C. Marland (1918-1965). Governor of West Virginia, 1953-1957.

Curt Warner (1962-). All-state football player at Pineville High School, All-American at Penn State, all-NFL with Seattle.

Bibliography

Bowman, Mary Keller. *Reference Book of Wyoming County History.* Parsons, McClain Printing Co., 1965.

Writers' Program. West Virginia. Pineville, Where Wyoming Trails Cross. Charleston, 1940. (Folk Studies, no. 9).

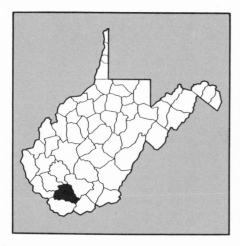

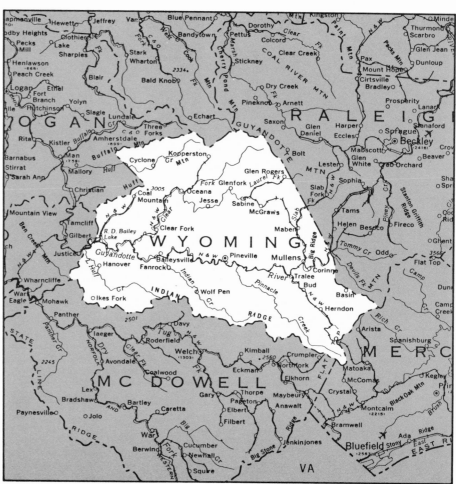

ECONOMIC PROFILE

Poverty status	
(all persons)	27.9%
65 and older	16.4%
Farms/value of farm products sold	53/$124,000
Retail sales	$78.95 million
Home ownership	80.5%
Value added by mining	$145.5 million
Median home value	$34,300
Median rent	$164/mo.

WYOMING COUNTY

Land in square miles	502
Total population	28,990
Percentage rural	100
Percentage female population	51.4
Percentage African-American population	0.8
Median age	33.6
Birth rate per 1,000 pop.	11.5
Percentage 65 and older	10.9
Median family income	$20,730

Educational attainment

Percent high school graduate or higher	53.0
Percent bachelor's degree or higher	6.2

UNITED STATES

Land in square miles	3.54 million
Total population	248,709,873
Percentage rural	24.8
Percentage female population	51.1
Percentage African-American population	12.1
Median age	33.1
Birth rate per 1,000 pop.	16.7
Death rate per 1,000 pop.	8.6
Percentage 65 and older	12.5
Median family income	$35,225

Educational attainment

Percent high school graduate or higher	75.2
Percent bachelor's degree or higher	20.3

WEST VIRGINIA

Land in square miles	24,119
Total population	1,793,000
Percentage rural	63.9
Percentage female population	51.9
Percentage African-American population	3.1
Median age	35.4
Birth rate per 1,000 pop.	12.6
Death rate per 1,00 pop.	10.6
Percentage 65 and older	15.0
Median family income	$25,602

Educational attainment

Percent high school graduate or higher	66.0
Percent bachelor's degree or higher	12.3

Appendix I

West Virginia's Ranking Among the 50 States *(1990 data unless indicated otherwise)*

Item	Rank	West Virginia	U.S.
Total population	34th	1,793,477	248,718,000
Land area (square miles)	41st	24,119	3,539,295
Population per square mile	26th	74.46	70.33
Percent change in population, (1980-1990)	50th	-8.00%	9.78%
Median age (1993)	2nd	36.2	33.7
Population 65 years old and over (1993)	5th	15.27%	12.71%
Non-white population	45th	3.8%	16.9%
Black population	34th	3.1%	12.1%
Asian and Pacific Islander	48th	0.4%	2.9%
American Indian, Eskimo, and Aleut	49th	0.1%	0.8%
Birth rate (per 1,000 population, 1992)	50th	12.2	16.0
Death rate (per 1,000 population, 1992)	1st	11.1	8.5
Marriage rate (per 1,000 population, 1992)	48th	6.8	9.3
Divorce rate (per 1,000 population, 1992)	17th	5.4	4.8
Physicians (per 100,000 population, 1992)	34th	194.42	244.39
Community Hospitals (per 100,000 population, 1992)	14th	5.15	2.07
Total housing units	34th	781,295	102,263,678
Home ownership rate (1992)	2nd	73.3	64.1
Crime rate (per 100,000 population, 1992)	50th	2609.7	5660.2
State prisoner incarceration rate (per 100,000 population, 1992)	48th	97	303
Public elementary and secondary schools Expenditures per capita (1991)	41st	$755.72	$863.19
Current expenditures per pupil (1994)	12th	$5,782	$5,314
Public school teachers' salaries (1993)	30th	$31,428	$36,846
Public high school graduation rate	18th	77.52%	71.19%
Per capita state and local government revenue (1991)	38th	$3,605.64	$4,286.81
Percent below poverty level (1992) Persons	3rd	22.3%	14.5%
Percent of eligible population reported voting in 1992	43rd	57.3%	61.3%
Per capita federal highway funds (1994)	14th	$87.66	$66.96
Energy consumption per capita (million BTUs, 1991)	6th	435	322

The 55 West Virginias - Index

Smith, George, 103
Smith, Howard W., 3
Smith, Governor Hulett C., 89
Smith, James, 69
Smith, Captain John, 81
Smith, Phil, 106
Smoke Hole Caverns, 24, 77
Smoke Hole Lodge, 24
Snead, Samuel J., 27
Snowshoe Ski Resort, ix
Snyder Knob, 90
Solus, 93
Sophia Knob, 89
South Branch (Potomac), 24, 25, 28, 32, 77, 102
South Charleston, 40, 41
Southern Methodists, 41
Spencer, 91, 95
Spencer Hospital, 95
Spruce Knob, 77 (illus)
Staggers, Harley O., 61
Standard Oil Company, 118
Stansbury, Harry A., 89
Starr, Blaze (see Fleming, Fannie Bell)
Stark Brothers Nurseries, 16
Starkey, Kay, 106
State Seal, 18
State Normal School at Marshall College, 12
Steamboats, 64
Steber, Eleanor, 76
Steel, 10, 30
Steer Creek, 14
Stephen, General Adam, 4
Stephenson, David, 46
Stephenson, James M. (home), 116 (illus)
Stevenson, Governor William E., 118
Stifel Family, 24
Stone Coal, 88
Stone Coal Creek, 44
Stonewall Jackson Lake Project, 45
Strother, David H., 5
Stroud, Adam, 110
Stroud's Creek, 110
Stump, Admiral Felix B., 118
Stumptown, 14
Stutler, Boyd, 14
Stydakar, Joe, 35
Summers County, 97-98
Summers, George W., 97
Summers, Lewis, 71
Summersville, 71
Summersville Reservoir, 71
Sutherland, Senator Howard, 91
Sutton, 8
Sutton Reservoir, 8
Sutton, John D., 8
Swain, George T., 48
Swisher, H. L., 29
Syracuse University, 65

T
Tams, 88
Tanners Crossroads, 95

Taylor County, 99-100
Taylor, John, 99
Tazewell County (VA), 48, 56, 58
Teague, Marj, 118
Terra Alta, 84
Tennessee, ix
Thompson, Phillip, 42
Tomlinson, Joseph, 52
Torytown, 4 (illus)
Trans-Allegheny Lunatic Asylum (see Weston Hospital), 44
Treaty of Greenville, 106
Trees, Joseph C., 112
Trout, Abraham, 108
Tucker County, ix, 90, 102, 103
Tucker, Henry St. George, 102
Tug Fork River, 56
Turkey Run, 106
Tutweiler, Edgar, 21
Twin Falls State Park, 119 (illus)
Tygart River, 2, 50, 81, 90, 99
Tygart, David, 90
Tyler County, 18, 78, 104-105, 112
Tyler County High School, 104
Tyler, Governor John, 104

U
Underwood, Governor Cecil, v., 104
Underwood, Mrs. Hovah, v.
Union, 18, 67
United Mine Workers of America, 42
University of Charleston, 41
University of Kentucky, 10
University of Pittsburgh, 91
US Supreme Court Boundary Marker, 24 (illus)
Upshur County, 44, 90, 106-107
Upshur, Abel Parker, 106

V
Vance, Cyrus, 35
Vandal, Abraham, 20
Vandalia, 20
VanDiver, Willard D., 33
Van Meter, George, 25
Van Meter, John, 28
Van Winkle, Senator Peter G., 118
Vernon, 30
Virginia, ix, 4, 6, 8, 10, 12, 22, 24, 26, 28, 32, 40, 54, 56, 64, 73, 77, 79, 88, 102, 106, 110, 112, 116
Virginia Electric and Power Company Plant, 24 (illus)
Virginia, Restored Government of, 73
Virginian Railway, 87

W
Warner, Curt, 119
Washington and Jefferson College, 75, 118
Washington, Booker T., 43
Washington, Charles, 38
Washington, George, 4, 24, 32, 36, 38, 54, 69
Watoga State Park, 82
Watson, Senator Clarence W., 51

Wayne, 108
Wayne County, 108-109
Wayne, General Anthony, 108
Webster County, ix, 90, 110-111
Webster, Daniel, 110
Webster Springs, 110
Weelin, 74
Welch, 56, 57
Welch, Captain Isaiah, 56
Weir, Ernest, 30
Weir Family, 30
Weirton, 30
Weirton High School, 10
Weirton Steel Corporation, 10, 30
Weiss, William, 76
Wells, Alexander, 10
Wells, Delilah, 104
Wells, Sarah, 104
Wells Inn, 104 (illus)
Wellsburg, 10
West, Jerry, 43
West Augusta, 64, 73
West Fork River, 14, 34, 44, 45, 50
West Liberty Academy, 75
West Liberty State College, 75
West Union, 18
West Virginia Agricultural College, 64
West Virginia Central and Pittsburgh Railway, 70, 102, 110
West Virginia Coal and Coke Railway, 8
West Virginia, Creation of State, 64
West Virginia Folk Festival, 22
West Virginia Institute of Technology, 20
West Virginia Northern Community College, 75
West Virginia Penitentiary, 52
West Virginia Pulp and Paper Company, 60
West Virginia School for the Deaf, 28
West Virginia School for the Blind, 28
West Virginia State College, 42
West Virginia State Seal, 18
West Virginia University, 20, 25, 60, 64, 65, 66
West Virginia University Institutue of Technology, 20
West Virginia Wesleyan College, 89, 106, 107, 117
Weston, 44, 106
Weston & Gauley Bridge Turnpike, 8 (illus)
Weston Hospital, 44
Wetzel County, 112-113
Wetzel, John, 52
Wetzel, Lewis, 53, 114
Wheeler, Billy Edd, 6
Wheeling, 40, 52, 73, 84, 99
Wheeling Jesuit University, 75
Wheeling Suspension Bridge, 73 (illus)
White, Albert B., 118
White, D. B., 6
White, Israel C., 65
White Sulphur Springs, 26
Whitesville, 6